Wayward Puritans

Allyn and Bacon
Boston · London · Toronto · Sydney · Tokyo · Singapore

Wayward Puritans

A Study in the Sociology of Deviance

KAI T. ERIKSON

A Simon & Schuster Company
Needham Heights, Massachusetts 02194

Library of Congress Catalog Card Number: 66-16140
Printed in the United States of America

ISBN 0-02-332200-4

5   96 95

Preface

IN EARLY 1630, when the first Puritan settlers of Massachusetts Bay were still making their way across the Atlantic, Governor John Winthrop delivered a thoughtful sermon to his fellow passengers. "We must consider," he warned them,

> that we shall be as a City upon a Hill, the eyes of all people are upon us; so that if we shall deal falsely with our god in this work we have undertaken and so cause him to withdraw his present help from us, we shall be made a story and a by-word through the world.[1]

The travelers who heard these words on the decks of the flagship Arabella could well appreciate the urgency in Winthrop's voice. They were a chosen company of saints, carrying a commission from God to cleanse the churches of Christ throughout the world by restoring them to the purity and simplicity they had known in the days of the Apostles. The impulse which brought these early immigrants across four thousand miles of ocean, then, was primarily one of revival, looking back all the way to Biblical times for its basic models and sanctions. Winthrop and his associates intended to build a new Israel in the

[1] John Winthrop, "A Model of Christian Charity," *Winthrop Papers* (Boston: The Massachusetts Historical Society, 1931), II, p. 295.

forests of Massachusetts, a Bible state of such compelling virtue that it would reform all Christianity by example. And so the members of the expedition began life in America with the clear understanding that they were making history.

The New England Puritans did "make history," and in a most dramatic way. We honor them as founders of a new civilization and celebrate their ocean voyage as if it had been the first flourish of an emerging American spirit, but in doing so we sometimes give them credit for a kind of success they did not in the least want to achieve. For these remarkable pioneers never meant to abandon England or retire by themselves into a world of their own. They hoped to establish New England as the spiritual capital of Christendom, the headquarters of the Protestant Reformation, and in this ambition they felt very much engaged in the mainstream of European life. In many respects, the passengers on board the Arabella and her sister ships were traveling to the outer edges of the known world in order to become more closely and more meaningfully related to events taking place at its center.

Eventually, of course, the New England Puritans lost contact with Europe and turned their extraordinary energies to the land which spread out before them in an unending plain. But it was many years before they were able to regard the place they had settled as a homeland or the lives they had lived as events in a local history; and during this interval the people of the Bay were almost suspended in time and place, gradually losing their old identity as Englishmen but not yet aware of their new one as Americans. The "eyes of all people" did not remain long on New England, and throughout the first three generations of settlement, the Puritans found themselves more and more remote from the world they were trying to refashion.

Because of its relative isolation, Massachusetts Bay offers an exceptional laboratory for social research. Somehow the colony seems to stand out from its European background, separated from those broader currents of history which make the scale of life in other parts of the seventeenth-century world appear larger and more complex. We are not dealing with nations or dynasties, here, but with small groups of men whose names we remember and whose lives we know something about, and so the history of the Bay has a fineness of texture and detail which is missing elsewhere. Moreover, the period is richly documented. It is unusual for a community this small to have become the focus of so much attention, but the subsequent history of the Bay made it a natural object of scholarly interest and the Puritans them-selves played a leading role in the process by keeping useful records of the holy experiment in which they were engaged. Although they would scarcely have approved of the approach taken in this study, or any other like it, the Puritans were always aware that their colony might one day serve as a test case for theories about society.

The purpose of the following study is to use the Puritan community as a setting in which to examine several ideas about deviant behavior. In this sense the subject matter of the book is primarily sociological, even though the data found in most of its pages are historical; and since this kind of interdisciplinary effort often raises a number of methodological issues, we might pause for a moment to consider how the two fields are related.

According to an honored tradition of scholarship, sociologists are people who study the general outlines of society, the "laws" governing social life, while historians are people who study those special moments in the past which have shaped the character of a given age or tempered the course of future events. Now this distinction between the "general" interests of the sociologist and the "particular" interests of the historian has been in vogue for many years and has furnished both fields with a convenient set of credentials. But when it is used to characterize a given piece of research, the distinction seems to lose much of its the-oretical crispness. After all, human events themselves are neither general nor particular until some student arranges them to fit the logic of his own approach, and in this day of interdisciplinary thinking it is no simple matter to say how the interests of the sociologist differ from those of the historian. Few sociologists who enjoy looking for data in the records of the past would want to pretend that they are moved by different enthusiasms or drawn to different conceptual problems than the historian, and it seems evident that a similar blurring of boundaries is taking place in the older of the two fields as well.

Yet there is one respect in which the following study should be viewed as sociological rather than historical. The data presented here have *not* been gathered in order to throw new light on the Puritan community in New England but to add something to our understanding of deviant behavior in general, and thus the Puritan experience in America has been treated in these pages as an example of human life everywhere. Whether or not the approach taken here is plausible from a historical point of view will eventually depend on the extent to which it helps explain the behavior of other peoples at other moments in time, and not just the particular subjects of this study.

Beyond this distinction, little attempt has been made in the study to draw a formal line between sociology and history. Some chapters, like the one which opens the study, deal almost exclusively with sociological matters, while others are chiefly devoted to a straightforward kind of historical reporting. All of the chapters, however, lie in a border area which can and probably should be claimed by both fields, and it should be a sufficient introduction to point out that the study was written by a sociologist in the interests of pursuing a sociological idea.

Accordingly, the book begins with a discussion of sociological theory and moves from there into historical analysis. Chapter 1 suggests that deviant forms of behavior are often a valuable resource in society, providing a kind of scope and dimension which is necessary to all social life. Chapter 2 follows with some background material on the Puritan settlers and the colony they built on the edge of the wilderness. From that point to the end of the study, three different themes extracted from the introductory argument will be discussed in turn as the narrative follows the colonists through their early years in America and notes how they dealt with their wayward countrymen. Chapter 3 looks at three "crime waves" which took place during the first century of settlement and tries to suggest that the styles of deviation a people experiences have something to do with the way it visualizes the boundaries of its cultural universe. Chapter 4 attempts to compute crime rates for one corner of the colony in order to test the notion that the number of deviant offenders a community can afford to recognize is likely to remain stable over time. Chapter 5, finally, reviews the Puritan attitude toward deviation and asks whether the ideological views which once sustained this attitude remain an important part of the context in which we deal with deviant behavior in our own day.

Thus the first two chapters can be read as separate introductions, the first presenting the ideas which give the book its underlying motif and the second presenting the historical characters whose lives and fortunes are the book's data. Each of the subsequent chapters, then, deals with a different implication of the introductory essay, using historical materials to illustrate and clarify the sociological argument.

The story of Massachusetts Bay has been told many times. The first formal history of the colony was published only twenty-five years after the original landing, and every generation since has offered its own version of those remarkable times. Yet the closeness of all this attention has somehow served to blur rather than sharpen the main outlines of the story, almost as if the facts had lost their more distinct features under the pressure of constant handling and had emerged looking like the misty figures of folklore instead. This should not be surprising, really, for the Puritans were almost a mythical people in their own day, not only because their manners were so easily caricatured, but also because they treated life with an exaggerated sense of mystery and always felt they were involved in a special cosmic drama. Yet the vagueness of the story also owes something to the many historians who have studied it—seventeenth-century settlers who wrote about their own age as if it were already historic, eighteenth-century scholars who tried to come to grips with this difficult inheritance, and nineteenth-century antiquarians who gathered every scrap of information on the period as if they were collecting exhibits for a museum of national history. One can hardly read through this shelf of material without wondering how many of these historians were looking for legends even when the facts themselves were explicit enough, trying to invent a mythical past for a nation which was far too young and far too self-conscious to have acquired one by the ordinary passage of time.

Historians know a great deal about this kind of myth-making and know how to see it as a form of historical data in its own right, but the sociologist needs to be very careful in these unfamiliar waters. For that reason, the following study relies as widely as possible on court records and other kinds of original document: these the sociologist can treat essentially as he would contemporary data, for they are the voices of the Puritans themselves speaking of the world in which they lived. Beyond this, however, the sociologist must depend on those secondary sources which happen to make the best sense to him, and here, too, he runs into a serious theoretical difficulty. For historians and sociologists use different criteria to decide which facts are most relevant to the problem at hand, and unless the sociologist is aware of this when he borrows from the work of historians, he runs the risk not only of writing second-rate history but second-rate sociology as well. Perhaps all one can do about the problem is to state as clearly as possible where his main dependencies lie. The bibliography at the end of the study lists those works which have been consulted most regularly and the footnotes scattered throughout the text should indicate the source of other debts;

but special mention should be made of Perry Miller, whose writings have had a deep influence on the whole of the study.

A brief word might be added about Puritan language. After considerable hesitation, I have decided to modernize the spelling of seventeenth-century quotations appearing in the text. This practice has the obvious drawback of leaving the reader unfamiliar with the style of the original, but it has the important advantage of making these passages easier to read. Throughout the study we will be more concerned with the content than with the style of the records anyway, and these alterations will at least reduce the danger that some reader might lose the thread of argument while pausing to make out the meaning of a difficult phrase.

Moreover, a good case can be made that this practice is wholly consistent with the spirit in which the passages were originally written. The Puritans of New England observed few systematic rules of spelling or grammar, composing their lines according to the rhythm of their own thoughts rather than to any logical pattern of syntax. Above all, they strove to be understood, and to this extent they might well have approved any efforts on the part of a modern editor to make their sentences more comprehensible to a new audience.

Only in rare instances have other liberties been taken with the original. On several occasions I have reduced capital letters when I thought they were particularly awkward, and two or three times I have changed a misleading bit of punctuation. If excuses are necessary for doing so, I need only point out that this privilege has been exercised by many editors before—so many, in fact, that it is quite impossible to know whether the eccentricities of style and punctuation which one finds in these early publications are the work of a Puritan author in Boston or a printer's apprentice in London.

.   .   .   .

It is always difficult for an author to keep meaningful accounts of the debts he incurs in the writing of a book, mainly
because the most important lessons he learns from his teachers
and colleagues are those which more or less slip into his consciousness without leaving any kind of permanent record behind.
The scholars mentioned here have all read the manuscript in one
or another stage of preparation and have contributed a great
deal to its style and content. Yet my thanks to them goes well
beyond this service, for the ideas on which the book is based
emerged from hours of conversation with these persons and have
been continually sharpened by my contacts with them.

The following persons have read drafts of the manuscript
and have offered me very helpful advice: Peter M. Blau, James
A. Davis, Bernard C. Holland, Elihu Katz, John I. Kitsuse,
Walter D. Love, Nelson W. Polsby, Geoffrey A. Sharp, Anselm
L. Strauss, Charles E. Strickland, and Robert L. Vosburg.

It happens that I have had the rare good fortune throughout
the writing of this book to review its contents with Erik H.
Erikson: the finished work has profited greatly from the counsel
he gave and the discussions we shared. I cannot easily measure
the debt I owe to Ray L. Birdwhistell, but I would like to pay
tribute to his extraordinary understanding of human behavior
and thank him for many generosities.

Most important, however, this book owes its existence to
Henry W. Brosin's respect for scholarly endeavors. Although the
material in these pages comes from old historical records and
describes a community of people who lived three hundred years
ago, the bulk of the study was written while I was on the faculty
of a modern, highly progressive medical school. It takes a certain
insulation to write about the seventeenth century in a setting
so urgently committed to the twentieth, and this insulation was
provided by Dr. Brosin in his capacity as Chairman of the
Department of Psychiatry, University of Pittsburgh School of

Medicine. I am grateful to him not only for the opportunity to do this study but for many helpful criticisms as well.

Morris Janowitz edited the book with a sensitive eye for questions of continuity and style and improved the final product considerably.

Finally, I have learned in the past four years why authors are usually so quick to mention their wives in acknowledgments of this sort. Joanne Erikson has contributed to this book in countless ways, but I will use this space only to thank her for those late hours when she listened to the eighth and ninth draft of a troublesome passage with the same humor and intelligence as she did the first.

KAI T. ERIKSON

Department of Psychiatry
Emory University
October, 1965

Contents

1 On the Sociology of Deviance *1*

2 The Puritans of Massachusetts Bay *31*

Historical Background *33*
The Puritan Ethos *43*
Law and Authority *54*

3 The Shapes of the Devil *65*

The Antinomian Controversy *71*
The Quaker Invasion *107*
The Witches of Salem Village *137*

4 Stabilities and Instabilities in Puritan Crime Rates *161*

5 Puritanism and Deviancy *183*

Appendix *207*

Bibliography *217*

Index *225*

1

On the Sociology of Deviance

IN 1895 Emile Durkheim wrote a book called *The Rules of Sociological Method* which was intended as a working manual for persons interested in the systematic study of society. One of the most important themes of Durkheim's work was that sociologists should formulate a new set of criteria for distinguishing between "normal" and "pathological" elements in the life of a society. Behavior which looks abnormal to the psychiatrist or the judge, he suggested, does not always look abnormal when viewed through the special lens of the sociologist; and thus students of the new science should be careful to understand that even the most aberrant forms of individual behavior may still be considered normal from this broader point of view. To illustrate his argument, Durkheim made the surprising observation that crime was really a natural kind of social activity, "an integral part of all healthy societies."[1]

Durkheim's interest in this subject had been expressed several years before when *The Division of Labor in Society* was first

[1] Emile Durkheim, *The Rules of Sociological Method*, trans. S. A. Solovay and J. H. Mueller (Glencoe, Ill.: The Free Press, 1958), p. 67.

published.[2] In that important book, he had suggested that crime (and by extension other forms of deviation) may actually perform a needed service to society by drawing people together in a common posture of anger and indignation. The deviant individual violates rules of conduct which the rest of the community holds in high respect; and when these people come together to express their outrage over the offense and to bear witness against the offender, they develop a tighter bond of solidarity than existed earlier. The excitement generated by the crime, in other words, quickens the tempo of interaction in the group and creates a climate in which the private sentiments of many separate persons are fused together into a common sense of morality.

Crime brings together upright consciences and concentrates them. We have only to notice what happens, particularly in a small town, when some moral scandal has just been committed. They stop each other on the street, they visit each other, they seek to come together to talk of the event and to wax indignant in common. From all the similar impressions which are exchanged, for all the temper that gets itself expressed, there emerges a unique temper . . . which is everybody's without being anybody's in particular. That is the public temper.[3]

The deviant act, then, creates a sense of mutuality among the people of a community by supplying a focus for group feeling. Like a war, a flood, or some other emergency, deviance makes people more alert to the interests they share in common and draws attention to those values which constitute the "collective conscience" of the community. Unless the rhythm of group life is punctuated by occasional moments of deviant behavior, presumably, social organization would be impossible.[4]

This brief argument has been regarded a classic of sociolog-

[2] Emile Durkheim, *The Division of Labor in Society*, trans. George Simpson (Glencoe, Ill.: The Free Press, 1960).

[3] *Ibid.*, p. 102.

[4] A similar point was later made by George Herbert Mead in his very important paper "The Psychology of Punitive Justice," *American Journal of Sociology*, XXIII (March 1918), pp. 577–602.

ical thinking ever since it was first presented, even though it has not inspired much in the way of empirical work. The purpose of the present chapter is to consider Durkheim's suggestion in terms more congenial to modern social theory and to see if these insights can be translated into useful research hypotheses. The pages to follow may range far afield from the starting point recommended by Durkheim, but they are addressed to the question he originally posed: does it make any sense to assert that deviant forms of behavior are a natural and even beneficial part of social life?

I

One of the earliest problems the sociologist encounters in his search for a meaningful approach to deviant behavior is that the subject itself does not seem to have any natural boundaries. Like people in any field, sociologists find it convenient to assume that the deviant person is somehow "different" from those of his fellows who manage to conform, but years of research into the problem have not yielded any important evidence as to what, if anything, this difference might be. Investigators have studied the character of the deviant's background, the content of his dreams, the shape of his skull, the substance of his thoughts—yet none of this information has enabled us to draw a clear line between the kind of person who commits deviant acts and the kind of person who does not. Nor can we gain a better perspective on the matter by shifting our attention away from the individual deviant and looking instead at the behavior he enacts. Definitions of deviance vary widely as we range over the various classes found in a single society or across the various cultures into which mankind is divided, and it soon becomes apparant that there are no objective properties which all deviant acts can be said to share in common —even within the confines of a given group. Behavior which qualifies one man for prison may qualify another for sainthood, since the quality of the act itself depends so much on the circumstances under which it was performed and the temper of the audience which witnessed it.

This being the case, many sociologists employ a far simpler tactic in their approach to the problem—namely, to let each social group in question provide its own definitions of deviant behavior. In this study, as in others dealing with the same general subject,[5] the term "deviance" refers to conduct which the people of a group consider so dangerous or embarrassing or irritating that they bring special sanctions to bear against the persons who exhibit it. Deviance is not a property *inherent in* any particular kind of behavior; it is a property *conferred upon* that behavior by the people who come into direct or indirect contact with it. The only way an observer can tell whether or not a given style of behavior is deviant, then, is to learn something about the standards of the audience which responds to it.

This definition may seem a little awkward in practice, but it has the advantage of bringing a neglected issue into proper focus. When the people of a community decide that it is time to "do something" about the conduct of one of their number, they are involved in a highly intricate process. After all, even the worst miscreant in society conforms most of the time, if only in the sense that he uses the correct silver at dinner, stops obediently at traffic lights, or in a hundred other ways respects the ordinary conventions of his group. And if his fellows elect to bring sanctions against him for the occasions when he does misbehave, they are responding to a few deviant details scattered among a vast array of entirely acceptable conduct. The person who appears in a criminal court and is stamped a "thief" may have spent no more than a passing moment engaged in that activity, and the same can be said for many of the people who pass in review before some agency of control and return from the experience

[5] See particularly the works of Edwin M. Lemert, Howard S. Becker, and John I. Kitsuse.

with a deviant label of one sort or another. When the community nominates someone to the deviant class, then, it is sifting a few important details out of the stream of behavior he has emitted and is in effect declaring that these details reflect the kind of person he "really" is. In law as well as in public opinion, the fact that someone has committed a felony or has been known to use narcotics can become the major identifying badge of his person: the very expression "he is a thief" or "he is an addict" seems to provide at once a description of his position in society and a profile of his character.

The manner in which a community sifts these telling details out of a person's overall performance, then, is an important part of its social control apparatus. And it is important to notice that the people of a community take a number of factors into account when they pass judgment on one another which are not immediately related to the deviant act itself: whether or not a person will be considered deviant, for instance, has something to do with his social class, his past record as an offender, the amount of remorse he manages to convey, and many similar concerns which take hold in the shifting mood of the community. Perhaps this is not so apparent in cases of serious crime or desperate illness, where the offending act looms so darkly that it obscures most of the other details of the person's life; but in the day-by-day sifting processes which take place throughout society this feature is always present. Some men who drink heavily are called alcoholics and others are not, some men who behave oddly are committed to hospitals and others are not, some men with no visible means of support are charged with vagrancy and others are not—and the difference between those who earn a deviant title in society and those who go their own way in peace is largely determined by the way in which the community filters out and codes the many details of behavior which come to its attention.

Once the problem is phrased in this manner we can ask: how does a community decide which of these behavioral details are important enough to merit special attention? And why, having made this decision, does it build institutions like prisons and asylums to detain the persons who perform them? The conventional answer to that question, of course, is that a society creates the machinery of control in order to protect itself against the "harmful" effects of deviation, in much the same way that an organism mobilizes its resources to combat an invasion of germs. Yet this simple view of the matter is apt to pose many more problems than it actually settles. As both Emile Durkheim and George Herbert Mead pointed out long ago, it is by no means evident that all acts considered deviant in society are in fact (or even in principle) harmful to group life. It is undoubtedly true that no culture would last long if its members engaged in murder or arson among themselves on any large scale, but there is no real evidence that many other of the activities considered deviant throughout the world (certain dietary prohibitions are a prominent example) have any relationship to the group's survival. In our own day, for instance, we might well ask why prostitution or marihuana smoking or homosexuality are thought to endanger the health of the social order. Perhaps these activities *are* dangerous, but to accept this conclusion without a thoughtful review of the situation is apt to blind us to the important fact that people in every corner of the world manage to survive handsomely while engaged in practices which their neighbors regard as extremely abhorrent. In the absence of any surer footing, then, it is quite reasonable for sociologists to return to the most innocent and yet the most basic question which can be asked about deviation: why does a community assign one form of behavior rather than another to the deviant class?

The following paragraphs will suggest one possible answer to that question.

II

Human actors are sorted into various kinds of collectivity, ranging from relatively small units such as the nuclear family to relatively large ones such as a nation or culture. One of the most stubborn difficulties in the study of deviation is that the problem is defined differently at each one of these levels: behavior that is considered unseemly within the context of a single family may be entirely acceptable to the community in general, while behavior that attracts severe censure from the members of the community may go altogether unnoticed elsewhere in the culture. People in society, then, must learn to deal separately with deviance at each one of these levels and to distinguish among them in his own daily activity. A man may disinherit his son for conduct that violates old family traditions or ostracize a neighbor for conduct that violates some local custom, but he is not expected to employ either of these standards when he serves as a juror in a court of law. In each of the three situations he is required to use a different set of criteria to decide whether or not the behavior in question exceeds tolerable limits.

In the next few pages we shall be talking about deviant behavior in social units called "communities," but the use of this term does not mean that the argument applies only at that level of organization. In theory, at least, the argument being made here should fit all kinds of human collectivity—families as well as whole cultures, small groups as well as nations—and the term "community" is only being used in this context because it seems particularly convenient.[6]

The people of a community spend most of their lives in close contact with one another, sharing a common sphere of experience which makes them feel that they belong to a special "kind" and live in a special "place." In the formal language of sociology, this means that communities are boundary maintaining: each has a specific territory in the world as a whole, not only in the sense that it occupies a defined region of geographical space but also in the sense that it takes over a particular niche in what might be

[6] In fact, the first statement of the general notion presented here was concerned with the study of small groups. See Robert A. Dentler and Kai T. Erikson, "The Functions of Deviance in Groups," *Social Problems,* VII (Fall 1959), pp. 98–107.

called cultural space and develops its own "ethos" or "way" within that compass. Both of these dimensions of group space, the geographical and the cultural, set the community apart as a special place and provide an important point of reference for its members.

When one describes any system as boundary maintaining, one is saying that it controls the fluctuation of its constituent parts so that the whole retains a limited range of activity, a given pattern of constancy and stability, within the larger environment. A human community can be said to maintain boundaries, then, in the sense that its members tend to confine themselves to a particular radius of activity and to regard any conduct which drifts outside that radius as somehow inappropriate or immoral. Thus the group retains a kind of cultural integrity, a voluntary restriction on its own potential for expansion, beyond that which is strictly required for accommodation to the environment. Human behavior can vary over an enormous range, but each community draws a symbolic set of parentheses around a certain segment of that range and limits its own activities within that narrower zone. These parentheses, so to speak, are the community's boundaries.

Now people who live together in communities cannot relate to one another in any coherent way or even acquire a sense of their own stature as group members unless they learn something about the boundaries of the territory they occupy in social space, if only because they need to sense what lies beyond the margins of the group before they can appreciate the special quality of the experience which takes place within it. Yet how do people learn about the boundaries of their community? And how do they convey this information to the generations which replace them?

To begin with, the only material found in a society for marking boundaries is the behavior of its members—or rather, the networks of interaction which link these members together in regular social relations. And the interactions which do the most

effective job of locating and publicizing the group's outer edges
would seem to be those which take place between deviant persons on the one side and official agents of the community on the
other. The deviant is a person whose activities have moved outside the margins of the group, and when the community calls
him to account for that vagrancy it is making a statement about
the nature and placement of its boundaries. It is declaring how
much variability and diversity can be tolerated within the group
before it begins to lose its distinctive shape, its unique identity.
Now there may be other moments in the life of the group which
perform a similar service: wars, for instance, can publicize a
group's boundaries by drawing attention to the line separating
the group from an adversary, and certain kinds of religious ritual,
dance ceremony, and other traditional pageantry can dramatize
the difference between "we" and "they" by portraying a symbolic
encounter between the two. But on the whole, members of a
community inform one another about the placement of their
boundaries by participating in the confrontations which occur
when persons who venture out to the edges of the group are
met by policing agents whose special business it is to guard the
cultural integrity of the community. Whether these confrontations
take the form of criminal trials, excommunication hearings,
courts-martial, or even psychiatric case conferences, they act as
boundary-maintaining devices in the sense that they demonstrate
to whatever audience is concerned where the line is drawn between behavior that belongs in the special universe of the group
and behavior that does not. In general, this kind of information
is not easily relayed by the straightforward use of language.
Most readers of this paragraph, for instance, have a fairly clear
idea of the line separating theft from more legitimate forms of
commerce, but few of them have ever seen a published statute
describing these differences. More likely than not, our information on the subject has been drawn from publicized instances in
which the relevant laws were applied—and for that matter, the
law itself is largely a collection of past cases and decisions, a

synthesis of the various confrontations which have occurred in the life of the legal order.

It may be important to note in this connection that confrontations between deviant offenders and the agents of control have always attracted a good deal of public attention. In our own past, the trial and punishment of offenders were staged in the market place and afforded the crowd a chance to participate in a direct, active way. Today, of course, we no longer parade deviants in the town square or expose them to the carnival atmosphere of a Tyburn, but it is interesting that the "reform" which brought about this change in penal practice coincided almost exactly with the development of newspapers as a medium of mass information. Perhaps this is no more than an accident of history, but it is nonetheless true that newspapers (and now radio and television) offer much the same kind of entertainment as public hangings or a Sunday visit to the local gaol. A considerable portion of what we call "news" is devoted to reports about deviant behavior and its consequences, and it is no simple matter to explain why these items should be considered newsworthy or why they should command the extraordinary attention they do. Perhaps they appeal to a number of psychological perversities among the mass audience, as commentators have suggested, but at the same time they constitute one of our main sources of information about the normative outlines of society. In a figurative sense, at least, morality and immorality meet at the public scaffold, and it is during this meeting that the line between them is drawn.

Boundaries are never a fixed property of any community. They are always shifting as the people of the group find new ways to define the outer limits of their universe, new ways to position themselves on the larger cultural map. Sometimes changes occur within the structure of the group which require its members to make a new survey of their territory—a change of leadership, a shift of mood. Sometimes changes occur in the surrounding environment, altering the background against which the people of the group have measured their own uniqueness. And always, new generations are moving in to take their turn guarding old institutions and need to be informed about the contours of the world they are inheriting. Thus single encounters between the deviant and his community are only fragments of an ongoing social process. Like an article of common law, boundaries remain a meaningful point of reference only so long as they are repeatedly tested by persons on the fringes of the group and repeatedly defended by persons chosen to represent the group's inner morality. Each time the community moves to censure some act of deviation, then, and convenes a formal ceremony to deal with the responsible offender, it sharpens the authority of the violated norm and restates where the boundaries of the group are located.

For these reasons, deviant behavior is not a simple kind of leakage which occurs when the machinery of society is in poor working order, but may be, in controlled quantities, an important condition for preserving the stability of social life. Deviant forms of behavior, by marking the outer edges of group life, give the inner structure its special character and thus supply the framework within which the people of the group develop an orderly sense of their own cultural identity. Perhaps this is what Aldous Huxley had in mind when he wrote:

Now tidiness is undeniably good—but a good of which it is easily possible to have too much and at too high a price. . . . The good life can only be lived in a society in which tidiness is preached and practised, but not too fanatically, and where efficiency is always haloed, as it were, by a tolerated margin of mess.[7]

This raises a delicate theoretical issue. If we grant that human groups often derive benefit from deviant behavior, can we then assume that they are organized in such a way as to promote this resource? Can we assume, in other words, that forces operate in the social structure to recruit offenders and to com-

7 Aldous Huxley, *Prisons: The "Carceri" Etchings by Piranesi* (London: The Trianon Press, 1949), p. 13.

mit them to long periods of service in the deviant ranks? This is not a question which can be answered with our present store of empirical data, but one observation can be made which gives the question an interesting perspective—namely, that deviant forms of conduct often seem to derive nourishment from the very agencies devised to inhibit them. Indeed, the agencies built by society for preventing deviance are often so poorly equipped for the task that we might well ask why this is regarded as their "real" function in the first place.

It is by now a thoroughly familiar argument that many of the institutions designed to discourage deviant behavior actually operate in such a way as to perpetuate it. For one thing, prisons, hospitals, and other similar agencies provide aid and shelter to large numbers of deviant persons, sometimes giving them a certain advantage in the competition for social resources. But beyond this, such institutions gather marginal people into tightly segregated groups, give them an opportunity to teach one another the skills and attitudes of a deviant career, and even provoke them into using these skills by reinforcing their sense of alienation from the rest of society.[8] Nor is this observation a modern one:

The misery suffered in gaols is not half their evil; they are filled with every sort of corruption that poverty and wickedness can generate; with all the shameless and profligate enormities that can be produced by the impudence of ignominy, the rage of want, and the malignity of dispair. In a prison the check of the public eye is removed; and the power of the law is spent. There are few fears, there are no blushes. The lewd inflame the more modest; the audacious harden the timid. Everyone fortifies himself as he can against his own remaining sensibility; endeavoring to practise on others the arts that are

[8] For a good description of this process in the modern prison, see Gresham Sykes, *The Society of Captives* (Princeton, N.J.: Princeton University Press, 1958). For discussions of similar problems in two different kinds of mental hospital, see Erving Goffman, *Asylums* (New York: Bobbs-Merrill, 1962) and Kai T. Erikson, "Patient Role and Social Uncertainty: A Dilemma of the Mentally Ill," *Psychiatry*, XX (August 1957), pp. 263–274.

practised on himself; and to gain the applause of his worst associates by imitating their manners.[9]

These lines, written almost two centuries ago, are a harsh indictment of prisons, but many of the conditions they describe continue to be reported in even the most modern studies of prison life. Looking at the matter from a long-range historical perspective, it is fair to conclude that prisons have done a conspicuously poor job of reforming the convicts placed in their custody; but the very consistency of this failure may have a peculiar logic of its own. Perhaps we find it difficult to change the worst of our penal practices because we *expect* the prison to harden the inmate's commitment to deviant forms of behavior and draw him more deeply into the deviant ranks. On the whole, we are a people who do not really expect deviants to change very much as they are processed through the control agencies we provide for them, and we are often reluctant to devote much of the community's resources to the job of rehabilitation. In this sense, the prison which graduates long rows of accomplished criminals (or, for that matter, the state asylum which stores its most severe cases away in some back ward) may do serious violence to the aims of its founders, but it does very little violence to the expectations of the population it serves.

These expectations, moreover, are found in every corner of society and constitute an important part of the climate in which we deal with deviant forms of behavior.

To begin with, the community's decision to bring deviant sanctions against one of its members is not a simple act of censure. It is an intricate rite of transition, at once moving the individual out of his ordinary place in society and transferring him into a special deviant position.[10] The ceremonies which mark

---

[9] Written by "a celebrated" but not otherwise identified author (perhaps Henry Fielding) and quoted in John Howard, *The State of the Prisons,* London, 1777 (London: J. M. Dent and Sons, 1929), p. 10.

[10] The classic description of this process as it applies to the medical patient is found in Talcott Parsons, *The Social System* (Glencoe, Ill.: The Free Press, 1951).

this change of status, generally, have a number of related phases. They supply a formal stage on which the deviant and his community can confront one another (as in the criminal trial); they make an announcement about the nature of his deviancy (a verdict or diagnosis, for example); and they place him in a particular role which is thought to neutralize the harmful effects of his misconduct (like the role of prisoner or patient). These commitment ceremonies tend to be occasions of wide public interest and ordinarily take place in a highly dramatic setting.[11] Perhaps the most obvious example of a commitment ceremony is the criminal trial, with its elaborate formality and exaggerated ritual, but more modest equivalents can be found wherever procedures are set up to judge whether or not someone is legitimately deviant.

Now an important feature of these ceremonies in our own culture is that they are almost irreversible. Most provisional roles conferred by society—those of the student or conscripted soldier, for example—include some kind of terminal ceremony to mark the individual's movement back out of the role once its temporary advantages have been exhausted. But the roles allotted the deviant seldom make allowance for this type of passage. He is ushered into the deviant position by a decisive and often dramatic ceremony, yet is retired from it with scarcely a word of public notice. And as a result, the deviant often returns home with no proper license to resume a normal life in the community. Nothing has happened to cancel out the stigmas imposed upon him by earlier commitment ceremonies; nothing has happened to revoke the verdict or diagnosis pronounced upon him at that time. It should not be surprising, then, that the people of the community are apt to greet the returning deviant with a considerable degree of apprehension and distrust, for in a very real sense they are not at all sure who he is.

[11] See Harold Garfinkel, "Successful Degradation Ceremonies," *American Journal of Sociology*, LXI (January 1956), pp. 420–424.

A circularity is thus set into motion which has all the ear-marks of a "self-fulfilling prophesy," to use Merton's fine phrase. On the one hand, it seems quite obvious that the community's apprehensions help reduce whatever chances the deviant might otherwise have had for a successful return home. Yet at the same time, everyday experience seems to show that these suspicions are wholly reasonable, for it is a well-known and highly pub-licized fact that many if not most ex-convicts return to crime after leaving prison and that large numbers of mental patients require further treatment after an initial hospitalization. The common feeling that deviant persons never really change, then, may derive from a faulty premise; but the feeling is expressed so frequently and with such conviction that it eventually creates the facts which later "prove" it to be correct. If the returning deviant encounters this circularity often enough, it is quite un-derstandable that he, too, may begin to wonder whether he has fully graduated from the deviant role, and he may respond to the uncertainty by resuming some kind of deviant activity. In many respects, this may be the only way for the individual and his community to agree what kind of person he is.

Moreover this prophesy is found in the official policies of even the most responsible agencies of control. Police depart-ments could not operate with any real effectiveness if they did not regard ex-convicts as a ready pool of suspects to be tapped in the event of trouble, and psychiatric clinics could not do a successful job in the community if they were not always alert to the possibility of former patients suffering relapses. Thus the prophesy gains currency at many levels within the social order, not only in the poorly informed attitudes of the community at large, but in the best informed theories of most control agencies as well.

In one form or another this problem has been recognized in the West for many hundreds of years, and this simple fact has a curious implication. For if our culture has supported a steady flow of deviation throughout long periods of historical

change, the rules which apply to any kind of evolutionary thinking would suggest that strong forces must be at work to keep
the flow intact—and this because it contributes in some important way to the survival of the culture as a whole. This does not
furnish us with sufficient warrant to declare that deviance is
"functional" (in any of the many senses of that term), but it
should certainly make us wary of the assumption so often made
in sociological circles that any well-structured society is somehow designed to prevent deviant behavior from occurring.[12]

It might be then argued that we need new metaphors to
carry our thinking about deviance onto a different plane. On the
whole, American sociologists have devoted most of their attention to those forces in society which seem to assert a central-
izing influence on human behavior, gathering people together
into tight clusters called "groups" and bringing them under the
jurisdiction of governing principles called "norms" or "standards." The questions which sociologists have traditionally asked
of their data, then, are addressed to the uniformities rather than
the divergencies of social life: how is it that people learn to
think in similar ways, to accept the same group moralities, to
move by the same rhythms of behavior, to see life with the same
eyes? How is it, in short, that cultures accomplish the incredible
alchemy of making unity out of diversity, harmony out of conflict, order out of confusion? Somehow we often act as if the
differences between people can be taken for granted, being too
natural to require comment, but that the symmetry which human groups manage to achieve must be explained by referring
to the molding influence of the social structure.

But variety, too, is a product of the social structure. It is
certainly remarkable that members of a culture come to look

[12] Albert K. Cohen, for example, speaking for a dominant strain in sociological thinking, takes the question quite for granted: "It would seem
that the control of deviant behavior is, by definition, a culture goal." See
"The Study of Social Disorganization and Deviant Behavior" in Merton, et
al., *Sociology Today* (New York: Basic Books, 1959), p. 465.

so much alike; but it is also remarkable that out of all this same-
ness a people can develop a complex division of labor, move off
into diverging career lines, scatter across the surface of the territory they share in common, and create so many differences of
temper, ideology, fashion, and mood. Perhaps we can conclude,
then, that two separate yet often competing currents are found
in any society: those forces which promote a high degree of
conformity among the people of the community so that they
know what to expect from one another, and those forces which
encourage a certain degree of diversity so that people can be
deployed across the range of group space to survey its potential, measure its capacity, and, in the case of those we call deviants, patrol its boundaries. In such a scheme, the deviant would
appear as a natural product of group differentiation. He is not
a bit of debris spun out by faulty social machinery, but a relevant figure in the community's overall division of labor.

III

The foregoing statement has introduced a number of different themes which lend themselves to one or another kind of
historical analysis, and the object of the present section will be
to draw attention to three of them. Each of these themes will
become the underlying motif of a later chapter as we begin to
apply the sociological argument to the historical example and
see whether it helps explain what happened in seventeenth century New England.

The first and most important theme has to do with the relationship between a community's boundaries and the kinds of
deviation experienced. Every human community has its own special set of boundaries, its own unique identity, and so we may
presume that every community also has its own characteristic
styles of deviant behavior. Societies which place a high premium
on ownership of property, for example, are likely to experience
a greater volume of theft than those which do not, while socie-

ties which emphasize political orthodoxy are apt to discover and punish more sedition than their less touchy neighbors. This obvious parallel occurs for at least two reasons. In the first place, any community which feels jeopardized by a particular form of behavior will impose more severe sanctions against it and devote more time and energy to the task of rooting it out. At the same time, however, the very fact that a group expresses its concern about a given set of values often seems to draw a deviant response from certain of its members. There are people in any society who appear to "choose" a deviant style exactly *because* it offends an important value of the group—some of them because they have an inner need to challenge this value in a direct test, and some of them, as Merton has pointed out, because they clumsily violate a norm in their very eagerness to abide by it.[13] In either of these events, the deviant and his more conventional counterpart live in much the same world of symbol and meaning, sharing a similar set of interests in the universe around them. The thief and his victim share a common respect for the value of property; the heretic and the inquisitor speak much the same language and are keyed to the same religious mysteries; the traitor and the patriot act in reference to the same political institutions, often use the same methods, and for that matter are sometimes the same person. Nor is this a trivial observation, for these pairs of adversaries are so well attuned to one another that they can and often do reverse roles with minor shifts in the historical climate. Joseph Conrad put the case very well in one of his novels when he described the policeman and the criminal as individuals "making countermoves in the same game": "Products of the same machine," he pointed out, "one classified as useful and the other as noxious, they take the machine for granted in different ways but with a seriousness essentially the same."[14]

[13] Robert K. Merton, *Social Theory and Social Structure* (Glencoe, Ill.: The Free Press, 1949).

[14] Joseph Conrad, *The Secret Agent* (New York: Doubleday Anchor, undated), pp. 68, 85.

The deviant and the conformist, then, are creatures of the same culture, inventions of the same imagination. And thus it can happen that the most feared and most respected styles of behavior known to a particular age often seem to mirror one another—so accurately, in fact, that observers looking in from another point in time cannot always tell them apart. A twentieth-century American, for example, is supposed to understand that larceny and other forms of commercial activity are wholly different, standing "on opposite sides of the law." A seventeenth-century American, on the other hand, if he lived in New England, was supposed to understand that Congregationalism and Antinomianism were as far apart as God and the Devil. Yet if we were to examine the contrasts of this sort which have been drawn in varying periods of the past or are currently drawn in other cultures than our own, we would find many of them rather obscure. It takes a keen theological eye to see where the Puritans drew the line between orthodoxy and some of the more serious forms of heresy, and it is quite conceivable that any Puritan who found himself transported to the middle of the present century would find it difficult to understand some of the distinctions we make, say, between proper and improper sexual conduct. Or to use a more current example, many Soviet commentators in our own day do not see any real difference between the forms of enterprise which put some Americans at the head of corporations and others in prison, while we, in our turn, cannot easily distinguish among the various shades of opinion which have meant the difference between life and death in the Soviet Union. Thus variations in action and attitude which mean "worlds of difference" at one time in history may seem like so many split hairs when exposed to the hard light of another.

At the height of the witchcraft hysteria in Massachusetts, the sociologist in Cotton Mather began to notice that the witches who terrorized the countryside were really very similar to the honest men who prosecuted them:

'Tis very remarkable to see what an impious and impudent imitation of divine things is apishly affected by the Devil, in several of those matters, whereof the confessions of our witches and the afflictions of our sufferers have informed us. . . . The witches do say, that they form themselves much after the manner of Congregational churches; and that they have a baptism and a supper, and officers among them, abominably resembling those of our Lord. . . . What is their striking down with a fierce look? What is their making of the afflicted rise, with a touch of their hand? What is their transportation thro' the air? What is their travelling in spirit, while their body is cast into a trance? What is their causing of cattle to run mad and perish? What is their entering their names in a book? What is their coming together from all parts, at the sound of a trumpet? What is their appearing sometimes clothed with light or fire upon them? What is their covering of themselves and their instruments with invisibility? But a blasphemous imitation of certain things recorded about our Savior or His Prophets, or the saints of the Kingdom of God.[15]

If deviation and conformity are so alike, it is not surprising that deviant behavior should seem to appear in a community at exactly those points where it is most feared. Men who fear witches soon find themselves surrounded by them; men who become jealous of private property soon encounter eager thieves. And if it is not always easy to know whether fear creates the deviance or deviance the fear, the affinity of the two has been a continuing course of wonder in human affairs. Observers of a later age may look back and understand that the witches and the magistrates were using the same cultural vocabulary and moving to the same cultural rhythms, but on the whole this secret is not known to the people of the time. To them, deviant behavior seems to come out of nowhere, an uninvited, perverse thrust at the very heart of the community. This feeling was caught nicely by one historian writing about deviance in the Bay colony:

[15] Cotton Mather, "Wonders of the Invisible World," in Samuel G. Drake, editor, *The Witchcraft Delusion in New England* (Roxbury, Mass.: W. Elliot Woodward, 1866), I, pp. 201–203.

Here we note a very natural relation between the spirit of persecution and the spirit which obstinately and even wantonly or perversely provoked it. The fathers were anxiously, we say morbidly and timidly, dreading lest their bold venture in the wilderness should be prostrated before it could strike root. . . . *Their troublers came precisely in the form and shape in which they apprehended them.* . . . As will soon appear, there was something extraordinary in the odd variety, the grotesque characteristics, and the specially irritating and exasperating course of that strange succession of men and women, of all sorts of odd opinions and notions, who presented themselves during a period of thirty years, seeming to have in common no other object than to grieve and exasperate the Puritan magistrates.[16]

The magistrates may well have been surprised by the form and shape in which their persistent troublers appeared, but these were only the forms and shapes of Puritan life itself—the reflected image of those values which stood at the core of the Puritan consciousness. Indeed, as we shall later see, it was during these meetings between the magistrates and their wayward countrymen that the forms of American Puritanism moved into focus, developed their own special character, and became the identifying landmarks of the larger community. In the process of defining the nature of deviation, the settlers were also defining the boundaries of their new universe, and this is the issue which shall provide the main focus of Chapter 3.

The second implication of the introductory essay which will be pursued in this study has to do with the *volume* of deviant behavior found in social life. It is one of the arguments of the present study that the amount of deviation a community encounters is apt to remain fairly constant over time. To start at the

[16] George Edward Ellis, "The Puritan Commonwealth: Its Basis, Organization, and Administration: Its Contentions; Its Conflicts with Heretics," in Justin Winsor, editor, *The Memorial History of Boston* (Boston: James Osgood, 1880), I, p. 166. Emphasis added.

beginning, it is a simple logistic fact that the number of deviancies which come to a community's attention are limited by the kinds of equipment it uses to detect and handle them, and to that extent the rate of deviation found in a community is at least in part a function of the size and complexity of its social control apparatus. A community's capacity for handling deviance, let us say, can be roughly estimated by counting its prison cells and hospital beds, its policemen and psychiatrists, its courts and clinics—and while this total cannot tell us anything important about the underlying psychological motives involved, it does say something about the manner in which the community views the problem. Most communities, it would seem, operate with the expectation that a relatively constant number of control agents is necessary to cope with a relatively constant number of offenders. The amount of men, money, and material assigned by society to "do something" about deviant behavior does not vary appreciably over time, and the implicit logic which governs the community's efforts to man a police force or maintain suitable facilities for the mentally ill seems to be that there is a fairly stable quota of trouble which should be anticipated.

In this sense, the agencies of control often seem to define their job as that of keeping deviance *within bounds* rather than that of obliterating it altogether. Many judges, for example, assume that severe punishments are a greater deterrent to crime than moderate ones, and so it is important to note that many of them are apt to impose harder penalties when crime seems to be on the increase and more lenient ones when it does not, almost as if the power of the bench were being used to keep the crime rate from getting out of hand.

Generally speaking, we invoke emergency measures when the volume of deviance threatens to grow beyond some level we have learned to consider "normal," but we do not react with the same alarm when the volume of deviance stays within those limits. As George Bernard Shaw once pointed out, a society completely intent on suppressing crime would punish every offender with all the severity it could manage—for the present system, with its careful attention to the formula that punishment should vary with the circumstances of the crime, only seems to suggest that society can afford certain kinds of crime more readily than others. From this point of view, every society acts on the assumption that it possesses the machinery for curbing crime—the power to impose inhibiting punishments—yet that power is ordinarily used in such a way as to stabilize rather than eliminate the amount of crime in the social order.

The same tendency toward stabilization can be seen in the field of mental health, where the number of available hospital beds and outpatient hours exercise a strict control over the number of people who are or can be regarded as sick. If the size of a hospital's waiting list grows too long, the only practical strategy is to discharge its present occupants more rapidly; and conversely, if the waiting list diminishes to the point where the hospital confronts a loss of revenue or a shortage of patients for teaching purposes, local practitioners are urged to send more referrals. In moments of severe pressure, perhaps, physicians may sometimes discharge a patient about whom they have private doubts, but the statistics of mental health do not record these reservations and the community is not ordinarily aware of them. When the community tries to assess the size of its deviant population, then, it is usually measuring the capacity of its own social control apparatus and not the inclinations toward deviance found among its members.

The reason for drawing attention to this logistic problem is not simply to point out that the community has poor measuring instruments for surveying the size of its deviant problem, but rather to suggest that the community develops its definition of deviance so that it encompasses a range of behavior roughly equivalent to the available space in its control apparatus—a kind of inverted Parkinson's law. That is, when the community calibrates its control machinery to handle a certain volume of deviant behavior, it tends to adjust its legal and psychiatric definitions of the problem in such a way that this volume is in fact realized. After all, every control agent and every control facility is "needed" by society. If the police should somehow learn to contain most of the crimes it now contends with, and if at the same time medical science should discover a cure for most of the mental disorders it now treats, it is still improbable that the existing control machinery would go unused. More likely, the agencies of control would turn their attention to other forms of behavior, even to the point of defining as deviant certain styles of conduct which were not regarded so earlier.

At any given time, then, the "worst" people in the community are considered its criminals, the "sickest" its patients, no matter how serious these conditions may appear according to some universal standard. In that sense, deviance can be defined as behavior which falls on the outer edge of the group's experience, whether the range of that experience is wide or narrow. In his earlier paper on the subject, Durkheim used an instructive example:

Imagine a society of saints, a perfect cloister of exemplary individuals. Crimes, properly so called, will there be unknown; but faults which appear venial to the layman will create there the same scandal that the ordinary offense does in ordinary consciousness. If, then, this society has the power to judge and punish, it will define these acts as criminal and will treat them as such.[17]

And much the same thing can be said about changes in the community as it moves from one period to another. If a community were able simply to lop off its most marginal people—banishing them to another part of the world, for instance, or executing them by the carload—it is unlikely that the volume of deviation in the community would really be reduced. Either new ranks of offenders would move into the vacuum in place of their departed fellows (as England discovered when it tried a policy of wholesale transportation to the colonies) or the agencies of

---

[17] Durkheim, *The Rules of Sociological Method*, pp. 68–69.

control would focus on a new target area and develop an interest in the behavior taking place there.

According to this argument, then, we should expect to find that the amount of deviation experienced by a community will remain fairly stable over time, and this is what we will look for in the material presented in Chapter 4.

The third implication of the introductory essay which will command further attention has to do with the way a society handles its deviant members. As has been suggested before, deviant persons can be said to supply needed services to society by marking the outer limits of group experience and providing a point of contrast which gives the norm some scope and dimension. Yet it is important to keep in mind that every society deals with this resource differently: each has its own method for naming people to deviant positions and its own method for deploying them across the range of group space. For the moment we may call these methods "deployment patterns" to indicate that they regulate the flow of deviant persons to and from the boundaries of the group and in this way govern the amount of deviation in the structure at any given time.

It cannot be the purpose of this study to make an inventory of the various deployment patterns known in different parts of the world, but we might note three which seem to reappear frequently in ethnological literature. First, there are societies which appoint special days or occasions as periods of general license, during which members of the group are permitted (if not expected) to violate rules they have observed during the preceding season and will observe again during the coming season. Second, there are societies in which deviance is regarded as a "natural" form of behavior for adolescents and young people generally, although individuals who take advantage of this exemption are expected to change their ways the moment they move

through defined ceremonies into adulthood. Finally, there are societies which have special clubs or orders whose stated business
it is to infringe the ordinary rules of the group in some prescribed
manner.

Now it might be argued that in each of these cases the re-
sulting behavior is entirely "expected" and therefore the product
of normative structuring: after all, the tribesman who curses the
gods and eats forbidden food during a festival is only responding to a new set of holiday rules, the youth who joins street riots
or profanes a sacred ceremony has a kind of permit from his
elders to behave in that fashion, and the "contrary" who obstinately refuses to follow the ordinary conventions of his group is
only doing what everyone expects of him anyway. Clearly, the
sanctions governing these departures from the norm suggest that
we are speaking of "deviance" in a rather special sense. Yet it
is one of the implications of this study that deviant behavior
in our own culture may be more tightly patterned than we ordinarily think, and while it may seem absurd to argue that people who act deviantly in our courts and clinics are responding
to "rules" in much the same sense as a participant in a festival,
it is still instructive to note the many parallels between these deployment patterns and the mechanisms at work in our own social order. All of these patterns allow people of the group an
intimate experience of the line separating morality from immorality; all of them exercise strict control over the volume of deviance found in the system at any given time—not because they
prevent it from occurring, to be sure, but because they can sched-
ule its appearance according to some cultural timetable. When
a group can halt a general period of license by declaring the end
of a festival, or transform rioting youths into responsible adults
by the use of a single rite of passage, it is demonstrating a remarkable degree of control. And perhaps we can look for similar mechanisms in other cultures where the "rules" governing
deviant behavior are not so apparent.

In any event, if we turn to the New England Puritans with

this thought in mind and ask how they regulated the human traffic moving in and out of provisional deviant roles, we may see the outlines of still another deployment pattern—one which may have left its imprint on our twentieth-century ways of dealing with the problem. This will be the main theme of Chapter 5.

These three different themes, then, will provide the theoretical frame for the chapters to follow. In Chapter 3 we will look at three "crime waves" which took place in the early years of the Bay colony and see how these episodes helped the settlers define the boundaries of their emerging society. Chapter 4 will examine a set of court records surviving from the time to look for evidence of stability in the local crime rate. Chapter 5, then, will turn to the Puritan "deployment pattern" and ask how this pattern influenced both the original settlers and later generations of Americans in their handling of deviant behavior.

But before we apply the sociological argument to the historical case, we should become better acquainted with the Puritans themselves and the settlement they built in the forests of New England.

2

The Puritans
of Massachusetts Bay

Historical Background

GRADE-SCHOOL histories often describe the New England Puritans as a band of refugees who flew from the persecution of their native land to found a new civilization in a remote corner of the world. The main theme of this story, however, does not really help us understand the Puritan settlement in America, for it pays too little attention to the English background against which the whole adventure was played. In order to imagine what this experience meant to the men who participated in it, we must begin by looking at the world they claimed as their own rather than the world they happened to make.

At the beginning of the sixteenth century, England was in the midst of a profound transition. The old social tapestry of the medieval world, with its tight patterns of corporate order and local authority, was giving way to the broader designs of the Renaissance. Power was draining out of country manors and into the hands of central administrations, ancient feudal loyalties were merging into a new kind of national patriotism, the brittle medieval class structure was beginning to shatter as new forms of commerce and new modes of thought were introduced into the growing towns. In a word, the whole scope and tempo of English social life was being refashioned on a national scale.

In the course of this transformation, the people of England began to feel a new restlessness reaching them inside the towns and castles, the convents and monasteries, which had sheltered them through the solitude of the middle ages, and they slowly came to recognize that they belonged to a larger order of things —a culture, a nation, a people. Men and women who had lived out their lives in deep provincial obscurity now emerged into an age of fresh possibilities, more alert to the currents of history around them and ready to take a more active interest in the events of the day. But there were few established platforms in England to give these expanding energies a focus or direction, few established parties to give them a voice. In many respects, a public was beginning to appear in England with no clear ideologies to claim its attention.

When Martin Luther issued his celebrated challenge to the Church in 1517, the reverberations were felt throughout the whole of the English countryside. The Lutheran doctrines provided a structure of debate which helped people organize their obscure feelings into statements of opinion, a set of issues which allowed them to gather into partisan camps. Indeed, the history of Tudor England, covering the rest of the sixteenth century, is largely a history of ideological realignment brought about by Reformation thinking: during this period a series of doctrinal lines was drawn through the populace, dividing it into parties and factions, denominations and sects, as the English people regrouped to fit the changing political scene.

The first of these lines made an abrupt appearance in 1533 when Henry VIII announced his break with Rome. It would be a mistake to assume that Henry's quarrel with the Pope split England into clear-cut Protestant and Catholic factions, as popular histories sometimes suggest, but it did act to sharpen the outlines of English thought by drawing a babel of different voices into two general modalities which later took Protestant and Catholic forms. Perhaps the most important outcome of Henry's action was to draw religious issues into the sphere of national policy, giving them a currency, a liveliness, well suited to the new mood of the country, and as a result the face of England assumed a secular look unlike that of any earlier age. By the end of Henry's long rule, the people of England had begun to participate in the life of their nation and expected to be consulted in matters concerning their own state religion. This was a condition which Mary Tudor was slow to understand during that tragic interlude when she tried to reinstate the Papal authority. But when Elizabeth came to the throne in 1558 she knew a truth her unhappy sister had never learned—that the people of England had become a force in politics and were no longer willing for issues of religious sovereignty to rest on the whim of each passing monarch.

Elizabeth tried to settle the issue at once. In the second year of her reign she persuaded Parliament to pass the Act of Supremacy and the Act of Uniformity, establishing the Church of England in roughly its present form, and this shrewd measure had the effect of diverting English loyalties into yet another set of camps. The Elizabethan settlement took a Protestant form by rejecting Rome entirely and by accepting Lutheran principles in many basic matters of creed; but at the same time it retained both the administrative machinery and the ceremonial superstructure of the older Catholic model. Elizabeth had chosen her position at the exact center of English opinion. Her compromise was broad enough to attract moderates of all persuasions, yet firm enough to leave the extreme positions on either flank without any real sources of support in the country; and thus the politics of the English Reformation were almost wholly realigned. The loyal Catholics on the right had little choice but to move underground, where they sulked in silence and occasionally broke out into petulant conspiracies against the crown;

but the more militant Protestants on the left were absorbed into the new structure and became a minority voice within the Church itself. These "Puritans," as the country soon called them, were Calvinists in temperament if not entirely in policy and shared a deep distrust of the Anglican hierarchy and its elaborate ritual apparatus. For all the differences among them, these early Puritans represented a hard new strain in English thought: strict in practice, intolerant in principle, austere in manner, they had seen the vision of a true church and were in no mood to let the Reformation come to a halt at this premature stage.

By the hard standards of the day, Elizabeth was quite tolerant in matters of religious opinion, and so long as she remained on the throne the Puritan movement was allowed to gather a slow momentum, drawing some support from the new commercial classes and even gaining a foothold in Parliament itself. More important, this interval gave the Puritan reformers a chance to develop a language of dissent and a style of persuasion which broadened their base of popular appeal considerably. For the moment, at least, the Puritans held their peace and continued to hope that by earnest argument and honest example they could still convert the Queen and the rest of the nation to their way of thinking.

This slender truce came to an end, however, when James I rode down from Edinburgh to accept his cousin's throne in 1603. James had a Scotsman's low opinion of English law and a Stuart's high opinion of royal authority, and between the two of these qualities he soon managed not only to stiffen the back of Puritan resistance but to earn the touchy distrust of Parliament as well. During the next twenty-five years, Parliament became more and more identified with Puritan interests and more and more resentful of the crown, until it finally abandoned its role as an organ of government to become an outright party of opposition. Slowly but surely, the men of Parliament and the men of the popular pulpit were gathering into an alliance which would carry England into the Civil Wars and the Commonwealth of

Oliver Cromwell. In 1625, when Charles I inherited his father's throne and his father's policies (but scarcely a trace of his father's occasional wisdom) the signs of conflict were everywhere apparent.

It was in this atmosphere that John Winthrop and his associates first considered a voyage to America. Protestant forces were losing ground all over the Continent, and although severe repression of the Puritans had not yet begun in England, Charles and his newly appointed Bishop of London had promised to turn their attention to that project in the near future. "All other churches of Europe are brought to desolation," Winthrop wrote about that time, "and our sins for which the Lord begins already to frown upon us and to cut us short, do threaten evil times to be coming for us." [1]

Few details are known about the arrangements made for this expedition, but even a bare outline of the story can tell us a great deal about the practical temper which lay below the surface of Puritan idealism. A group of prominent Puritans, largely from the eastern counties of Norfolk, Essex, and Suffolk, controlled a trading company which had acquired commercial rights to a large tract of land in New England. By a remarkable oversight, the charter granting these rights did not stipulate where the headquarters of the firm should be located, although every similar organization in the land kept its central office in one of the leading cities. We do not know whether that oversight was actually an accident or had been engineered by friends in court, but we do know that the group took unexpected advantage of it: they distributed the company's remaining shares among people who were planning to make the journey or willing to sponsor it, and simply set sail for America with the charter on board. In effect, they had moved an entire corporation—its books, offices, stockholders, and directors—to a new location outside the country and were preparing to use that business in-

[1] John Winthrop, letter to his wife, *Winthrop Papers*, II, p. 138.

strument as the basis for a civil government. The charter would serve as their title to the land and as their fundamental constitution; the officers of the company would act as their magistrates; the regular meetings of the stockholders would become their legislative sessions. John Winthrop was called "Governor" even before the party sailed from England, not because he anticipated election to that high office but because he occupied a position in the corporation equivalent to what we now designate as "chairman of the board." In any event, the charter gave the company jurisdiction over an enormous tract of land and authorized it to take whatever precautions were necessary for keeping discipline among its members and crew. This document provided the government of the Bay with its only legal claim for almost sixty years.

To an observer standing on the docks at Southhampton and watching the tiny fleet leave for America, the event was not a momentous one. It was an interesting spectacle, to be sure, a dramatic moment, but many another fleet had sailed out of the harbor to challenge the grey Atlantic, and in a land preoccupied with other troubles the departure of the Winthrop party was little more than a passing episode. On the whole, the Puritan cause in England was not greatly weakened by the emigration. Among the several hundred people who left England with the first fleet (and this is true of the fifteen to twenty thousand people who followed them to New England in the next decade) were a group of educated gentry and some of the most highly respected Puritan ministers in the country, but few of them had seen service in Parliament and none of them had been outstanding spokesmen for the Puritan movement on a national scale. Winthrop was a minor public official and owner of a respectable manor in Suffolk, a man of recognized quality but no unusual prominence, and most of his colleagues were of a similar stamp. Yet the sheer energy involved in the undertaking was impressive enough to raise a question among thoughtful people in the Puritan ranks, for it was already clear that men of such useful parts were needed at home to join the coming struggle —a problem which many a departing emigrant must have debated in the privacy of his own soul. When the fleet of four vessels finally left Southhampton in April, 1630, encouraged by the tone of John Cotton's departing sermon and full of hope for the future, a note of indecision still hung in the air. They were Englishmen leaving their native land, brethren leaving their congregations, Puritans defecting in time of trouble, men and women leaving their homes, families, friends, and careers. They were moving away from the only world they had known; and perhaps it is not surprising that many of them would begin to feel a double-edged concern that they were abandoning England, and that England, in its turn, was about to abandon them.

In other respects, too, the Winthrop party formed a special current even within the main flow of English Puritanism. During the early Stuart period, Puritan ambitions in England were primarily aimed at a national church along lines developed in Calvin's Geneva and then emerging in Presbyterian Scotland. But as this emphasis became more pronounced among leading Puritans, a number of splinter groups broke away from the main stem of the movement and began to develop variants of their own, beginning that process of fission which was later to scatter the Puritan brethren into a whole galaxy of different sects. Fragmentation had not yet taken place on a serious scale when Winthrop left for America, but already three separate moods (it was too early to call them parties) could be distinguished in Puritan thought. On the right flank were the more conservative Puritans who wanted to establish a national church on a Presbyterian model; on the left flank were the impatient Separatists who had carried the logic of their creed to its furthest conclusion and broken with the Church of England entirely (a small band of whom had been settled in Plymouth for ten years); and in the center, gathered together on a rather dubious platform, were a group of people shortly to be known as Congregationalists. By and large, as recent scholarship has suggested, the Winthrop party belonged to that middle position.[2]

The Congregationalists were developing two notions which divided them from their Presbyterian fellows. First, they were beginning to argue that the church should limit its membership to those "visible saints" who could demonstrate that they belonged to God's special elect. Second, they held that each individual congregation was a separately constituted unit, making its own covenant with God, choosing its own ministers, and free from the authority of any central church organization. Now these articles of faith represented a special problem to the more traditional Puritans. Like everyone else in the seventeenth-century, Puritans generally took it for granted that the church should be an instrument of national power and enforce religious uniformity with as heavy a hand as proved necessary; yet if the church were limited to visible saints, how could it assert any authority over the rest of the community? Even Calvin had estimated that only one out of every five persons in an ordinary population was destined for grace. And furthermore, if there were no central hierarchy in the church to supervise the activities of the various congregations, how could anyone hope to avoid the schism and independence of thought that would invariably follow? The Congregationalists felt sure that they had a convincing answer to these questions, of course, but they also knew that the proof could only come from a practical demonstration and not from an exercise in theological reasoning.

Puritans who shared a congregational outlook, then, found themselves in a difficult spot once the Church of England had been settled on a sure footing. They did not want to break away

[2] See particularly A. S. P. Woodhouse, *Puritanism and Liberty* (London: J. M. Dent, 1938), and Perry Miller, *Orthodoxy in Massachusetts* (Cambridge, Mass.: Harvard University Press, 1933).

from the established Church and join the Separatists in exile, yet at the same time they flatly objected to most of the principles on which that Church was founded. For a few years, at least, the problem was handled by a flow of carefully phrased position papers from the Puritan pulpit. The Church of England was a "true" church, the clergy explained, even though it continued to embrace some annoying errors; but so long as the brethren worked diligently to correct these errors, it was entirely proper for them to seek salvation within the orbit of the Church. "We make no separation from the Church," one elder had pointed out delicately, "we go about to separate in those things that offend in the Church, to the end that we, being knit to the sincere truth of the Gospel, might afterward in the same bond be more nearly and closely joined together." [3] The problem with this reasoning, as critics were more than happy to point out, was that the list of "errors" compiled by the Puritan reformers soon grew to epic length. For all practical purposes, the Congregationalists were insisting that the Anglican Church was wholly legitimate—save only that it had the wrong organization, the wrong ceremonies, the wrong members, and the wrong ministry. Needless to add, this was an impressive indictment to draw against any "true" church.

It is hardly surprising that such a position would fail to convince critics. Pamphleteers representing every shade of Protestant opinion began to complain that the Congregationalists should show their true colors and retire from the Church—the Anglicans because they wanted to embarrass the Puritan movement in general, the Presbyterians because they wanted to disengage themselves from at least this one brand of nonconformity, and the luckless Separatists because they needed any allies they could persuade (or shame) into joining them. And so the Congregationalists found themselves in an almost preposterous position. In order to defend their loyalty to the established

---

[3] Thomas Cartwright, quoted in Miller, *Orthodoxy*, p. 69.

Church, they not only had to act on principles which offended their deepest religious sensitivities but also had to repudiate the only people in England who agreed with them on most fundamental matters of doctrine.

One obvious solution to the dilemma, of course, was a dignified and orderly retreat. Congregationalists would find it far more convenient to stay within the Church spiritually if they were removed from it physically, carrying their notions about worship into a distant land where their declarations of loyalty could be heard but their actual practices could not be observed. However much this thought figured in the final decision, Winthrop and others of his party were careful to point out that they were not leaving the Church. As has been suggested, the slender legality of their charter made it difficult for them to say anything else; but it is also important to remember that the spokesmen of the group were English gentlemen, loyal to the traditions of their class and instinctively reluctant to defy constituted authority. It is interesting to speculate what roles these men might have played had they remained in England long enough to witness the Civil Wars, for some of them would have cut strange figures sitting on the benches of Parliament or around the campfires of Cromwell's army; but whatever course they might have taken a decade later, they were, in the quieter days of 1630, little inclined to leave the King and his established Church.

"As for ourselves," wrote Thomas Shepard and John Allin after the company had been safely settled in Massachusetts, "we look not upon our departure to these parts to be a separation (rigidly taken) but a lawful succession, or a heavenly translation from the corrupt to more pure churches." [4]

This was the keynote to the early Puritan experience in

---

[4] Thomas Shepard and John Allin, "A defense of the answer made unto the nine questions or positions sent from New England against the reply thereto by Mr. John Ball," London, 1648, quoted in Miller, *Orthodoxy*, p. 150.

America. The new colony was to be a legal extension of old England but a spiritual revision of everything that was wrong at home. It was to be a "heavenly translation" of Puritan theory into a living community of saints, a blueprint for the City of God. In time, of course, the ideas which had generated the original venture were lost: generations grew up in the new world which had lost all contact with the old, and before long the hopeful utopia had been transformed into a confident nation which no longer measured its accomplishments on an English yardstick. The later sons of Massachusetts knew far more about the forests and the seas than they did about old Archbishop Laud, and in their hands the Puritan sense of grace lost its mistier qualities and became the determined realism of the Yankee.

In the meantime, the first generation of settlers began to clear away the underbrush and to build in its place a living monument to the Word of God, a practical demonstration that men could govern themselves on earth exactly as He intended that they should. Before we try to understand the character of this holy experiment, however, we should consider in fuller detail who these original settlers were.

The Puritan Ethos

One of the difficulties with written history is that it describes events far more systematically than they were originally experienced. Often, it is only after the tide of history has swept out a government or changed old ways of thinking that we see any pattern in the events by which change was accomplished, and then we are apt to write as if that pattern had been evident from the beginning. There are times, however, when it is important to recognize that events only assume a distinct shape after they have taken place and that the people who experience them do not sense the outlines which seem so apparent to us later. This is particularly true when we turn to the Puritan "ethos" or "world view." The Puritan reformers in England began an upheaval which changed the face of the modern world, and we naturally look for a logic in that course of events—a *movement* or *cause* to give the drama its motive force. Yet we are likely to misunderstand the underlying strength of Puritanism in its early days if we look too narrowly at its formal structure and overlook its subjective appeal. Puritanism in England was a deep religious mood before it became a creed or platform: indeed, the real failure of Puritanism on both sides of the Atlantic may have been that this mood could not be translated into dogma without losing much of its native force and vigor. When we talk about Puritanism in the years before the Civil Wars, then, we are discussing an emotional tone as well as a body of theory, an ideological stance as well as a political program; and it is important to realize that the tone and the stance were difficult to understand even during the age when they were most profoundly felt.

Originally, "Puritan" seems to have been a term of derision, applied rather loosely to people who expressed some dissatisfaction with the workings of the established Church. Because the scope of these objections was sometimes quite trivial, the term came to suggest an argumentative, stubborn frame of mind, a cheerless concern with technicalities. Elizabeth herself had complained that Puritans "were over-bold with God Almighty, making too many subtle scannings of His blessed will, as lawyers do with human testaments." [5] And another observer noted in 1623:

I find many that are called Puritans; yet few, or none, that will own the name. Whereof the reason sure is this, that 'tis for the most part held a name of infamy; and is so new, that it hath scarcely yet obtained a definition: nor is it an appellation derived from one man's name, whose writings we may find digested in a volume: whereby we do much err in the application. . . . One will have him one that

[5] "Queen's Proclamation Against Non-Conformists," 1573. Quoted in Ralph Barton Perry, *Puritanism and Democracy* (New York: Vanguard Press, 1944), p. 37.

lives religiously and will not revel it in a shoreless excess. Another, him that in some tenets only is peculiar. Another, him that will not swear. Absolutely to define him is a work, I think, of difficulty. Some I know rejoice in the name; but more sure they be such as least understand it. As he is more generally in these times taken, I suppose we might call him a Church-Rebel, or one that would exclude order that his brain might rule.[6]

To many Englishmen of the period, then, Puritanism represented an annoying exaggeration of conventional values, much like the fundamentalism of our own day. Whatever the particular hue of their discontent, the Puritans seemed to lack an ordinary sense of humor and an ordinary sense of proportion because of their obstinate readiness to challenge the authority of the Church and to "fill the world with brawls about undeterminable tenets." [7]

To the early Stuart Kings, however, these theological eccentricities had a particularly sinister ring. The gentlemen of the coffee houses might scorn the Puritans as a group of cranky, contentious men, but James I and Charles I thought they could see a deep menace in those sober ranks. Puritanism meant to them a religious denomination, a political party, a revolutionary force—in each of these respects a clear danger to the throne. Yet even when royal feeling was most pronounced on the subject, few members of the King's official household, let alone the people of the country generally, could say who the Puritans were or what they were up to. In 1620, for example, a correspondent in Dublin wrote to a friend in court requesting that the King make some effort to define this word "Puritan" so that the conversion of the Irish might continue in peace:

I hope you are not ignorant of the hurt that has come to the Church by this name, Puritan, and how his Majesty's good intent and meaning therein is much abused and wronged; and especially in this poor coun-

---

[6] Owen Felltham, "Resolves: Divine, Moral, Political," 1623. Found in *Seventeenth Century Prose,* edited by Peter Ure (London: Penguin Books, 1956), II, pp. 94–95.

[7] *Ibid.,* p. 95.

try where the Pope, and Popery, is so much affected. . . . [The priests here] have now stirred up some crafty Papists, who very boldly rail both at [Anglican] ministers and people, saying they seek to sow this damnable heresy of Puritanism among them, which word, though not understand, but only known to be odious to his Majesty, makes many afraid of joining themselves to the Gospel . . . so to prevent greater mischief that may follow, it were good to petition his Majesty to define a Puritan, whereby the mouths of these scoffing enemies would be stopped.[8]

It is not surprising that James would find it difficult to "define a Puritan," no matter how acutely he sensed a danger to his throne from that quarter, for many of the men who later found themselves caught up in the excitement of the Civil Wars were not sure what brought them there. The Puritan movement was manned by a vast assortment of people: they met together for the first time in the early 1640's, stayed together long enough to take the field against their King, and then began to splinter off into the various directions from which they had come, each of them driven by his own private visions and disciplined by his own private convictions. It was no easy matter for a contemporary observer, nor is it now for a later historian, to understand who these people were or where they eventually went.

The group which emigrated to Massachusetts Bay, however, seems to have been fairly homogeneous in matters of religious doctrine. The thinking of these New England saints has been discussed in a number of excellent works, most notably in the writings of Perry Miller,[9] and thus the notes which follow will be less concerned with the formal content of Puritan theory than with the "world view" this theory helped create.

Although Puritanism was known in its own day as a "dangerous novelty," the original tone of the movement suggested revival far more than it did reform. Generally speaking, the

[8] Letter from Emmanuel Downing to James Ussher, 1620, *Collections of the Massachusetts Historical Society,* Fourth Series, II, pp. 120–121.

[9] See particularly *The New England Mind: The Seventeenth Century* (New York: Macmillan, 1939).

Puritan's faith began with a primitive kind of nostalgia. As a Christian, he longed for an intimate experience of grace, a chance to touch and be touched by God directly; and since he felt frustrated in this design by the strict formalities of the Church, he learned to resent most of the religious institutions invented by society to mediate between God and men. He saw the ritual and ornamentation of the Church service as so much foliage obstructing his view of God, the intricate hierarchy of the organized Church as little more than an elaborate filter through which his expressions of piety had to be strained. To the extent that he had any policies at all, then, the Puritan wanted to restore the church to the simplicity it had known in the days of the Apostles: he wanted to choose his own words in prayer, to worship in a plain setting, to scrape away the decorations and insignia, the rules and formulae, which had formed like a crust over the primitive core of Christianity. This is presumably what our observer had meant when he described the Puritan as a man who "would exclude order that his brain might rule."

Yet this observation is not wholly fair, for the Puritans had an instrument of authority to offer which governed their lives as firmly as all the bishops in Christendom—the Holy Writ itself. Perhaps the most important difference between the Puritans and their Anglican countrymen was that they regarded the Bible a complete guide to Christian living, a digest of all the statutes and regulations necessary for human government. The Scriptures not only supplied rules for the broader issues of church polity but for the tiniest details of everyday life as well, and many Puritans were fully capable of demanding that a clergyman remove some emblem from his vestments unless he could justify the extravagance by producing a warrant for it from the pages of the Bible. This, in turn, is what Elizabeth had meant when she likened the Puritans to lawyers and complained of their narrow literality: it often seemed that the Puritans were paying more attention to the footnotes than to the main text of human experience.

Like most revivals, Puritanism did not begin as an organized creed at all. So long as it remained a profound sense of piety shared among a few believers and encouraged by the popular pulpit, Puritanism had a certain freshness and vitality which proved immensely appealing; but when this subjective frame of mind was translated into statements of principle, it became the thorny dogma which James had so much difficulty understanding. The tensions which fed the Puritan's deep longing for grace, the conflicts which sharpened his extraordinary discipline, the anxieties which drove him into a constant fear of sin—all these inner strains looked like so many contradictions when converted into figures of language. It was an emotional and an ideological tone which could not be easily written down on paper.

The first Puritans to reach Massachusetts never saw the contradictions in their theory (nor would they have worried about it if they had) and continued to feel that their position was derived from the soundest logic. But it is important to understand that the essential strength of that logic lay in the conviction that truth had been forever discovered in its entirety. Puritan logic was not a method for learning the truth; it was a rhetorical means for communicating it to others. The twentieth-century reader who tries to feel his way through the mists of Puritan argument may sooner or later decide that it is nothing more than a versatile display of sophistry, but he then must remind himself that men who already *know* the truth have scant need for the niceties of inductive reasoning. The truth as seen by the Puritans was wholly clear. God had chosen an elite to represent Him on earth and to join Him in Heaven. People who belonged to this elite learned of their appointment through the agency of a deep conversion experience, giving them a special responsibility and a special competence to control the destinies of others. People who had never been touched by this moment of grace could have no idea what conversion meant, and thus were simply not qualified to teach the truth or share in the government of men. This is only one of several respects in which seventeenth-century Puritanism seems to anticipate the main spirit of nineteenth-century Marxism: neither the reprobates of the one period nor the bourgeoisie of the other were really capable of appreciating the truth, no matter how earnestly or sympathetically they tried, and so for their own good they must submit to the superior insight of those who did.

Despite the conservatism and intellectualism of so much of their scholarship, the Puritans were sometimes remote from the political drifts of their own age, living in a kind of cultural suspension. To begin with, they had drawn away from many of the cultural landmarks which give each people a sense of their place in human history and human society—the folklore and traditions, the art and literature, the monuments and memories which become a part of their national identity. But beyond this, the Puritans had little interest in or respect for the way in which men ordinarily view their own past. History, as they understood it, was largely a story of religious decline anyway, a weary chronicle of knights and princes, battles and kingdoms, which had no relation at all to the fundamental realities of existence. Reality did not belong to any particular time or place: it originated in the imagination of God, and man's only hope of coming to terms with this truth lay in the devotion of his whole attention to the one document in which God had reviewed His intentions.

The Bible was not just an announcement of God's purpose, however. It was a catalogue of all possible forms of human experience, a digest of history both past and yet to come. Events which occur in the lives of men and give them an illusion that time is passing in some orderly fashion are no more than echoes of thoughts in the mind of God, registered permanently in the Scriptures. And so the Puritan world took its form by analogy rather than by sequence of time. Everything that happens in the present world is only a flickering reproduction of something that has happened before, a repetition of some divine truth, and the Puritans assumed that they could discover the archetypes from which their own experience was derived by careful study of the world around them. In a very real sense, they knew that there is nothing new under the sun.

All of this makes the contradictions of Puritanism seem sharper, and when one considers the various themes that played through the Puritan's mind it becomes easier to understand the conclusion reached by so many of his English contemporaries— that the Puritan approach to life was a fabric woven almost entirely out of paradoxes.

The first paradox becomes apparent when one tries to place the Puritans in the historical context of their own age, for Puritanism seems to be at once a survival from the medieval past and a decided protest against everything that that past had represented. More than any other people of Protestant Europe, the Puritans drew their imagery from late medieval religion, sharing its pervading sense of doom, its desperate piety, and its anxious preoccupation with sin. Yet at the same time, they rejected most of the pageantry and festivity, the color and style, which had once acted to offset the harshness of that cosmology. We find the same fatalism in seventeenth-century Massachusetts as in fifteenth-century France, but nowhere do we see majestic cathedrals to offer sanctuary or joyful bells to soften the terror; nowhere do we see the spirit of a compassionate Virgin. In many ways the Puritans were the most direct descendants of the medieval tradition, but in other ways they were almost the last people in Europe to come to terms with that inheritance.

The second paradox is that the Puritans were able to combine a remarkable degree both of pride and humility in the same general frame. On the one hand, they are unworthy products of this sinful world, base creatures who wallow in greed and act contemptibly before their God. Yet on the other hand, these same creatures are fashioned in the image of angels and have been given a commission from God to convert the heathen, strike down the haughty, punish the sinful, and take upon themselves the authority of acting in His name. And so the Puritan always seems to be exhibiting a double nature. In his confessions he insists that he is worthless and contemptible, but in his professions he declares that it is his special privilege and obligation to challenge all the established traditions in Christendom. Humility is the badge of his sanctity; but sanctity, in turn, is his warrant for converting the whole world to his way of thinking. James I was quite sensitive to this ambivalence when he drew attention to

the preposterous humility of one of the proud Puritans . . . [who say], "We are all but vile worms, and yet will judge and give Law to our King, but will be judged or controlled by none." Surely there is more pride under such a one's black bonnet, than under Alexander the Great his diadem.[10]

The third paradox is that the Puritan outlook depended for balance upon a constant shift between conviction and uncertainty. The hard logic of their creed required the Puritans always to doubt the evidence of their own senses but never to doubt the fundamental precepts of their religion. Life was a long and often painful search for signs of grace: the seeker had to explore every corner of his own consciousness for signs of conversion, weighing his own thoughts, testing his own moods, probing his every impulse, permitting himself no relief from this self-scrutiny for fear that sin would seep into his soul when his guard was down. At times, the very simplicity of this search can be touching. "I am now forty years old," one mason from Quincy wrote in his diary,

and cannot but be ashamed to look back and consider how I have spent my lost time; being at a great loss whether any true grace be wrought in my soul or no: corruption in me is very powerful; grace (if any) is very weak and languid. . . .[11]

And at other times the gnawing uncertainty can erupt into a terrible violence, as John Winthrop reports in his journal:

A woman of the Boston congregation, having been in much trouble of mind about her spiritual estate, at length grew into utter despera-

---

[10] Basilikon Doron, 1599. Found in Charles H. McIlwain, editor, *The Political Works of James I* (Cambridge, Mass.: Harvard University Press, 1918), p. 38.

[11] Quoted in Charles Francis Adams, *Three Episodes of Massachusetts History* (Boston: Houghton Mifflin, 1903), III, p. 718.

tion, and could not endure to hear of any comfort, etc., so as one day she took her little infant and threw it into a well, and then came into the house and said, now she was sure she would be damned, for she had drowned her child. . . .[12]

One important effect of this insecurity, however, was to make the Puritan all the surer of the things he did know. The Bible told him the difference between right and wrong, and in his efforts to shape the world to those clear moralities he could be positively ferocious. Massachusetts was a society in which the very idea of intelligent controversy seemed absurd: after all, the truth was as plain as the print on everyone's Bible, and any soul capable of entertaining doubt after this truth had been interpreted for him by the godly clergy must either suffer from a crippling defect or be caught in the snares of Satan himself. If a persuasive argument should jar a Puritan's certitude or a clever line of reasoning confuse him, he had every right to suspect that some devilish mischief was afoot. One day the President of Harvard College, soon to be dismissed for his views on infant baptism, confided his thoughts to one of the leading ministers of the Bay. The latter wrote in his diary:

That day . . . after I came from him, I had a strange experience: I found hurrying and pressing suggestions against Paedobaptism, and injected scruples and thoughts whether the other way might not be right, and infant baptism an invention of men; and whether I might with good conscience baptise children and the like. And these thoughts were darted in with some impression and left a strange sickliness on my spirit. Yet, methought, it was not hard to discern that they were from the Evil One . . . And it made me fearful to go needlessly to Mr. D[unster]; for methought I found a venom and a poison in his insinuations and discourses against Paedobaptism.[13]

[12] John Winthrop, *History of New England*, edited by James K. Hosmer (New York: Scribner's, 1908), I, p. 230. Cited hereafter as Winthrop, Journal.

[13] Quoted in Brooks Adams, *The Emancipation of Massachusetts* (New York: Houghton Mifflin, 1919), second edition, p. 277. The minister in question was Jonathan Mitchell.

Doubt was indeed a "strange experience" for a Puritan saint, even if, as in the above case, he was one of the finest minds produced in the colony.

In general, then, the Puritan's world was made up of sharpened contrasts on all sides—and this gave him an extraordinary sensitivity to the miraculous. In this respect, too, the Puritans remind us of their medieval forebears. They had the same credulity, the same sense of wonder and mystery, the same ability to see hidden meanings in the rustling of a leaf, a sudden toothache, or some unexpected happening. The voices of God could be heard throughout nature, and the Puritans knew how to listen for them with all the awe of children.

But perhaps the most striking paradox of the New England experience (and the one most relevant to the present study) is that the inner materials of Puritan faith so often seemed inconsistent with the outer conditions this faith helped to promote. As we shall later see, Puritanism in the Bay eventually generated both a respect for individual freedom and a need for external discipline, a sense of personal privacy and a system of public accountability, a reliance on self-assertion and a belief in erratic fate. The main dilemma of Puritanism throughout the early years of settlement was to bring these discrepant sets of qualities together.

This discussion of paradoxes in the Puritan ethos brings to mind a passage by Erik H. Erikson:

It is commonplace to state that whatever one may come to consider a truly American trait can be shown to have its equally characteristic opposite. This, one suspects, is true of all "national characters," or (as I would prefer to call them) national identities—so true, in fact, that one may begin rather than end with the proposition that a nation's identity is derived from the ways in which history has, as it were, counterpointed certain opposite potentialities; the ways in which it lifts this counterpoint to a unique style of civilization, or lets it disintegrate into a mere contradiction.[14]

When the Puritans found themselves alone in the wilderness of New England, they had to find some way to strike a balance between these sets of paradoxes and yet to combine them into a national identity which would reflect the holy commonwealth they had promised to establish. The Puritan experiment was an effort to join abstract theory with practical experience, to seek perfection in a decidedly imperfect world. The effort could not but produce discrepancy; and thus the major problem of the settlers was to create a set of government machinery which would represent both the highest ideals and the meanest expediencies of life in the new world, without permitting the difference between them to become "a mere contradiction."

Nowhere was this problem better illustrated than in the settlers' attempts to formulate a code of law.

Law and Authority

The legal structure of Massachusetts Bay was unusual in several important respects. It contained an odd assortment of ingredients, gathered from many different corners of the Puritan world and blended together in a very brief period of time. The law of Massachusetts had no time to mature gracefully, as had the common law of England, because it was designed for immediate use and because it combined elements which did not fuse easily at all: a dogma which drew most of its vigor from the militancy of the Old Testament and a political theory already sensitive to the traditional safeguards of English Law. The legal apparatus which emerged from this unlikely union, then, can

[14] Erik H. Erikson, *Childhood and Society* (New York: Norton, 1950), p. 244.

tell us a great deal about the Puritan's sense of discipline and his attitude toward the law.

It will be remembered that the government of Massachusetts Bay was first chartered as a business corporation with authority to exercise jurisdiction over the lands it now occupied. According to the charter, the company was to be managed by a Governor, a Deputy Governor, and a board of eighteen "Assistants" elected annually by the stockholders. This board, including its several officers, was to meet once a month in what might be called executive session to administer the ordinary business of the company. The larger body of stockholders, known as "freemen," was to meet four times a year in a General Court to admit new members, elect officers, and make regulations

for the good and welfare of the said company, and for the government and ordering of said lands and plantations, and the people inhabiting and to inhabit the same . . . so as such laws and ordinances be not contrary or repugnant to the laws and statutes of England.[15]

For all practical purposes, this was the basic framework within which the first settlers were to construct their commonwealth. The actual terms of the charter do not seem particularly restrictive at first, considering that the colonists were asked only to observe the laws of their own country, but the Puritans who landed on the shores of Massachusetts were not at all sure that their experiment could be fashioned even within those generous limits. And so the early history of the Bay was marked by a continuing controversy about the place of civil law in a religious community. Right at the beginning the settlers had to face an issue which was implicit in the ideological luggage they had brought with them across the ocean. Puritanism had been gen-

[15] Records of the Governor and Company of the Massachusetts Bay in New England, edited by Nathaniel B. Shurtleff (Boston: Printed by order of the Massachusetts Legislature, 1853–54), I, p. 12. Cited hereafter as Massachusetts Records.

erated in England as a stance of opposition to the established order of things, and in the process it had developed a style of propaganda and a sense of tactic which were in many respects better suited to disputing the existing law than writing it anew. Somehow the mood of protest that had nourished the Puritan movement throughout its earlier days would have to be converted into a new kind of party loyalty and discipline.

Moreover the new arrivals were not very experienced in matters of jurisprudence. For one thing, common law was beginning to emerge in England as the final successor to the prerogative courts and the various forms of Roman Law, but this transition had been so recent and its implications so poorly understood that few persons on either side of the Atlantic could say with any confidence what "the laws and statutes of England" really were. Coke had just begun to compile his authoritative *Institutes,* Parliament would not meet again until 1641; and during this eventful pause in English history people favoring different legal traditions were preparing for a final contest to determine what the law of the land should be. In addition, there were few persons among the original group of settlers who knew very much about constitutional law. The legal ideas which moved across the Atlantic with the first wave of immigrants, then, were a ragged assortment indeed: a few basic articles of common law, some knowledge of specific statutes, and a rough familiarity with custom and usage as it had developed in various local jurisdictions throughout England.[16]

But far and away the most important source of Puritan legal thinking was the Bible itself. A good deal of controversy has taken place among historians about the extent to which later

[16] See the following: George L. Haskins, *Law and Authority in Early Massachusetts* (New York: Macmillan, 1960); Julius Geobel, Jr., "King's Law and Local Custom in Seventeenth Century New England," *Columbia Law Review,* XXXI (1954); and Zechariah Chafee, Jr., "Introduction," *Records of the Suffolk County Court, 1671–1680* (Boston: Publications of the Colonial Society of Massachusetts, 1933).

Puritan law was actually derived from the Scriptures, but there can be little doubt that the original settlers intended to base their legal structure almost wholly on Biblical authority. This was, after all, one of the main objects of the whole experiment—to prove that the Word of God could serve as a competent basis for human government as well as a guide to the usual business of life.

Yet this honest program proved a little awkward in practice. When the Word was read from the pulpit it seemed to provide a crisp set of rules for men to walk by, but when it was brought into court to judge the ordinary run of civil and criminal cases it no longer seemed so exact. For all its commanding tone, the Bible had few passages which could be read as statutes; and even when the law of God was spelled out in the plainest detail it was difficult to know what penalties were appropriate for each particular offense. Thus the Puritan courts were caught up in a constant tangle of inference and interpretation: What punishment is proper for persons convicted of burglary? Should attempted murder be tried as a capital crime? Does the law against adultery apply when an English settler is found lying with an Indian woman? Every day the courts seemed to discover some frightful new sin for which there was no precedent in Biblical history, and on each of these occasions the leaders of the community would have to rummage deep into their libraries and deep into their memories for some ruling to cover the emergency.

When problems of this sort are raised in a secular court they are referred to professional jurists who are presumed to have some special wisdom about the meaning of the law, but when the law in question is considered divine, the only available experts are ordained ones. During the first years of the colony, accordingly, it was the ministers who settled most questions of law, acting in their capacity as accredited Bible scholars. Whenever the court encountered a circumstance not explicitly covered in the Scriptures, it would ask a panel of local clergymen to "set a rule" for the issue at hand—and some of the briefs sub-mitted to the court were formidable documents indeed.

This arrangement was exactly what the leaders of the party had promised when they declared their intention of shaping a "due form" of government for both church and state. The magis-trates would act as a secular arm in the service of the church, keeping order among the populace so that the gospel could be taught in peace and safety, while the ministers would provide the final authority for most questions related to longer-range policy. On the whole, the settlers accepted this division of labor with no unusual feelings of alarm, but the use of the Bible as a legal code created two sources of friction which were to affect the future of the colony in decisive ways.

The first problem was that the use of clerical opinion in cases before the bench was in many ways contrary to the spirit (if not the letter) of English law. It is a fundamental principle of common law that a statute can furnish rules only for cases within its immediate purview and cannot be used as the basis for ana-logical thinking. That is, a statute which stipulates some penalty for theft cannot be used to punish usury or extortion, no matter how similar those crimes may appear from another point of view. Yet the Bible could be used as an instrument of law only if the ministers and magistrates allowed themselves a generous leeway in drawing analogies and making inferences, since the Judaic Code was simply not specific enough to supply rules for each offense. As we shall see in the next chapter, for example, one of the few detailed charges brought against Anne Hutchinson dur-ing the Antinomian crisis was that she had violated the Biblical commandment to "honor thy father and thy mother," the apparent reasoning being that she had failed to offer proper deference to the "fathers" of the community. This principle of analogical think-ing was flatly stated in the Preface to the Code of 1648:

So soon as God had set up political government among His People Israel He gave them a body of laws for judgment both in civil and criminal causes. These were brief and fundamental principles, yet withall so full and comprehensive as out of them clear deductions were to be drawn to all particular cases in future time.[17]

We have no evidence that this practice proved embarrassing to the upper ranks of the Puritan leadership or caused any serious discomfort to the main body of settlers, but many of them must have felt a little uneasy about the legality of such a procedure, particularly since it was likely sooner or later to raise eyebrows among the careful parliamentarians in England.

The second problem arising from the use of the Bible as a source of law was that many thoughtful people in the colony soon became apprehensive because so many discretionary powers were held by the leading clique. Again, we have no reason to suspect that popular feeling ran against the theocratic outlines of the state, but it is clear that "the people" themselves (which in this instance really means the enfranchised stockholders) were anxious to obtain an official code of law; and so a constitutional battle opened which had a deep impact on the political life of the Bay. On one side stood the people, soon to be represented in the General Court by elected Deputies, who felt that the Bible would supply a clearer and safer guide to law if the elders would declare at the outset how they intended to interpret its more ambiguous passages. On the other side stood the ruling cadre of the community, the ministers and magistrates, who felt that the whole enterprise would be jeopardized if they were no longer able to interpret the Word as they saw fit. This was not a simple contest for power between an entrenched elite and an expanding middle class: it was an issue which touched the deepest nerves of Puritan theory and had an important bearing on the very structure of the holy commonwealth.

For all practical purposes, the battle lines had been drawn even before the party had sailed from England. It will be remembered that the trading company was controlled by a group of Puritans who either intended to make the journey themselves

[17] Quoted in Haskins, *Law and Authority,* p. 56.

or were willing to sponsor it in some active way. But it happened that of the hundred or more persons who owned stock in the corporation only a few actually emigrated with the first wave of settlers, and as a result there were no more than ten or eleven freemen on the American side of the Atlantic during the first year of the colony. These few men, of course, were all officers in the company, which meant that the two organs of government provided in the charter, the Court of Assistants and the General Court, were almost identical in composition. In a sense, every member of the electorate was already a magistrate. Throughout the early months of settlement, then, all legislative, judicial, and executive functions of government were shared by a compact handful of men.

In 1631 this cadre passed a resolution that each new candidate for citizenship must belong to a church in good standing, which meant in effect that he must be registered as a person of orthodox convictions. There is no sure way of knowing how many settlers qualified for the franchise on those grounds, but the records indicate that only some 1300 persons had been sworn in as freemen by the end of the first decade—almost surely a minority of the eligible males.[18] Thus the responsibilities of citizenship were vested in a select portion of the population, forming a class of people who could be relied upon to support the main principles of the larger enterprise; yet for all the unity of purpose found among the members of this body there was one area in which the original cadre and

[18] The estimate of 1300 comes from Haskins. There has been considerable debate among historians about the number of settlers who enjoyed the privileges of the franchise. The traditional estimate has been that around one-fifth of the populace were freemen, following the statement made by Thomas Lechford who visited the colony in its early years. In recent years, however, this assumption has been seriously questioned, mainly by B. Katherine Brown. See "A Note on the Puritan Concept of Aristocracy," *Mississippi Valley Historical Review*, XLI (1954), pp. 105–112 and "Freemanship in Puritan Massachusetts," *American Historical Review*, LIX (1954), pp. 865–883.

the newer ranks of freemen could rarely agree, and this had to do with the wisdom of publishing a formal code of law.

The leading men of the colony were faced with some delicate problems when the code first came up for consideration. To begin with, the charter had stated emphatically that the company should enact no statutes contrary to the laws of England, yet, as Winthrop readily admitted, the magistrates were preparing to do exactly that.[19] From a tactical point of view, at least, it seemed a little risky to put the colony's laws in written form where their deviation from English practice would be all the more visible to critics at home. Moreover, the idea of an official body of laws did not sit easily among the other tenets of Congregational theory. The New England saints were quite opposed to any form of central church hierarchy and were naturally anxious to protect the autonomy of each individual congregation. Like most men of the age, however, they did not think for a moment that the state should permit any diversity of opinion on matters of religious faith, and thus the founding generation had to find a way to keep the orthodoxy intact without imposing any external machinery of control on the various congregations. The New England method of maintaining discipline was based on private conferences, public prayers, and a whole network of other pressures which were nonetheless compelling because they were unofficial. In such a scheme, of course, there would be little room for a secular code of law, for even if the ministers took a leading role in composing that code they would be binding one another to a formal structure of control and denying the "freedom" of the separate congregations. In a sense, then, the magistrates and ministers were arguing for local option in the face of central administration, much as advocates of "States' Rights" do in our own day—but with the very important difference that they expected each local unit of government to choose exactly the same course independently. The Congregationalists had always argued

[19] Winthrop, Journal, I, p. 323.

that a true community of saints could get along handsomely without a class of prelates to supervise their activities, since men who have pledged themselves to observe the Word of God will by definition conform to the same standards and agree on all important matters of policy. If this objective could be achieved, what value could there be in a written code of law? At best, it would weaken a profound article of Congregational creed and perhaps furnish ammunition for critics in England; at worst, it would provide a legal umbrella under which the unregenerate could hide their sins.

So Winthrop and others of the elite argued that the laws of Massachusetts Bay should develop gradually over time, "by practise and custom . . . as in our church discipline." [20] But advocates of the code remained unimpressed by Winthrop's reasoning, and by 1635 pressure had become so strong that the General Court ordered work on the code to begin.

The deputies having conceived great danger to our state, in regard that our magistrates, for want of positive laws, in many cases, might proceed according to their discretions, it was agreed that some men should be appointed to frame a body of grounds of laws, in resemblance to a Magna Carta, which, being allowed by some of the ministers, and the general court, should be received for fundamental laws.[21]

The project dragged heavily for several years, largely because the senior men were "not very forward in the matter," as Winthrop candidly tells us.[22] But in 1641 a brief bill of rights, known since as the Body of Liberties, was passed by the General Court, and in 1648 a comprehensive code of law was finally adopted. It was the first compilation of its kind in the English-speaking world.

A good deal has been written about these two editions of the code and we do not need to be detained by a review of their

[20] Winthrop, Journal, I, p. 324.
[21] Winthrop, Journal, I, p. 151.
[22] Winthrop, Journal, I, p. 324.

content. Indeed, the single fact that they were published at all is far more important than any of the specific articles they provided, for the code was the first in a long line of measures which acted to translate the subjective ethic of Puritanism into an objective statement of principle. And as was to happen so often in the early years of the commonwealth, the codification of Puritan theory only served to make its internal contradictions seem all the more apparent. When a settler found himself before a court of law, he was confronted by two quite different traditions of justice—the cautious safeguards of the common law, on the one side, and the sharp, retributive tone of the Old Testament on the other. These drifts in the Puritan consciousness could lie side by side so long as they were not brought to the surface at the same time, but when they were both written into a formal code of law, the discrepancy between them became rather awkward. A judge can hardly be expected to respect the careful protections of common law if he sees himself as God's vengeful prosecutor, nor could a man before the bar be expected to conduct a reasoned defense if he were denied counsel and had spent the preceding night in the company of ministers trying desperately to "reduce him to the truth."

The author of the code was Nathaniel Ward, a retired minister who seemed to reflect this contradiction in his own person. Ward was a man with sure Puritan instincts—intolerant, severe, utterly convinced of his own election. Yet at the same time he was a traveled man of the world with a good deal of experience in court and some background in law. The choice of this man to write the code was surely no accident: New England practice required that a clergyman oversee the drafting of a legal code and draw most of his materials from Biblical sources, but for that purpose alone there were several ministers in the Bay with better credentials than Ward, and in fact there is some evidence that John Cotton, easily the most respected clergyman in New England, wrote an alternative draft of the code that was rejected by the General Court. Ward brought a complex background to the task of codifying law, and it is reasonable to assume that the General Court, in selecting him for the assignment, was responding as much to his experience in English law as to his knowledge of scriptural texts.

Edmund Morgan has written that "the code was not merely a bill of rights to protect the inhabitants of Massachusetts from arbitrary government. It was a blueprint of the whole Puritan experiment, an attempt to spell out the dimensions of the New England way." [23] But it proved extremely difficult to assemble all the different fragments of that "way" into a single blueprint. Like all utopias, Massachusetts had to carry along a good deal of what was old in the process of starting anew: by accepting the Bible as their spiritual parentage, England as their political parentage, and a trading company as their economic parentage, the colonists of the Bay owed their corporate identity to a wide assortment of elements. In the beginning, at least, the price the colonists had to pay for their effort to gather these old scraps of doctrine and new threads of experience into a coherent social fabric was to be doubly self-conscious of who they were and where they were going.

It is quite natural, then, that they would seek new frames of reference to help them remember who they were; and it is just as natural that they would begin to look with increasing apprehension at the activities of the Devil. One of the surest ways to confirm an identity, for communities as well as for individuals, is to find some way of measuring what one is *not*. And as the settlers began to take stock of themselves in this new and uncertain land, they learned to study the shapes in which the Devil appeared to them with special care—for he had always loomed in Puritan imagery as a dark adversary against which people could test the edge of their own sainthood.

[23] Edmund S. Morgan, *The Puritan Dilemma—The Story of John Winthrop* (Boston: Little, Brown, 1958), p. 170.

3

The Shapes of the Devil

But ye are a chosen generation, a royal priesthood, an holy nation, a peculiar people . . . which in time past were not a people, but are now the people of God. (I Peter 2:9,10)

DURING the first six decades of settlement in Massachusetts, three serious "crime waves" occurred which affected the young colony in decisive ways. Each of these waves became an object of wide public concern and each of them drew large numbers of deviant offenders. In the long chapter to follow, we will look at these episodes in turn to see what impact they had on the emerging outlines of the Puritan commonwealth. The narrative will try to argue that the Antinomian controversy of 1636, the Quaker persecutions of the late 1650's, and the witchcraft hysteria of 1692 were three different attempts by the people of the Bay to clarify their position in the world as a whole, to redefine the boundaries which set New England apart as a new experiment in living.

When the New England Puritans put an entire ocean between themselves and the rest of the world, they were declaring

in effect that issues of the most profound gravity divided them
from their contemporaries at home. They had voyaged many
miles to establish a new model of Christian fellowship, an ethic
they could call the "New England Way," and it was naturally
important to them that this ethic have a clear enough character
to stand out from other ideologies and other programs in the
world of the time. The New England Way was to represent their
uniqueness as a people, their justification for withdrawing into
the empty spaces of America; it was to be their history, their
folklore, their special emblem, their destiny. Throughout the
early years of settlement, then, as shifts in the political climate
of Europe changed the background against which the colony
measured its own particular character, the people of the Bay
had to review again and again what qualities distinguished them
from the rest of mankind. It would be quite a few years before
they began to regard the land they had settled as a nation: New
England was not a "place" to them but a "way," not a country
but an experimental proving ground in which a new kind of
religious spirit could be tested and developed. And this meant
that the settlers had to be extremely thoughtful about the political
and religious institutions they were building in their wilderness
home, for they knew that the identifying mark of their "way"
would only be seen in the architecture of their commonwealth:
in the form of their government, the organization of their church,
the tenor of their law.

The following pages will be concerned with the first theme
introduced in Chapter 1, that whenever a community is confronted by a significant relocation of boundaries, a shift in its
territorial position, it is likely to experience a change in the kinds
of behavior handled by its various agencies of control. The occasion which triggers this boundary crisis may take several forms—
a realignment of power within the group, for example, or the
appearance of new adversaries outside it—but in any case the
crisis itself will be reflected in altered patterns of deviation and
perceived by the people of the group as something akin to what

we now call a crime wave. These waves dramatize the issues at stake when a given boundary becomes blurred in the drift of passing events, and the encounters which follow between the new deviants and the older agents of control provide a forum, as it were, in which the issue can be articulated more clearly, a stage on which it can be portrayed in sharper relief.

Now this general hypotheisis must be qualified in two important ways. First, when one argues that boundary crises are apt to set "crime waves" into motion, one is suggesting two things —that the community begins to censure forms of behavior which have been present in the group for some time but have never attracted any particular attention before, and that certain people in the group who have already acquired a disposition to act deviantly move into the breach and begin to test the boundary in question. For the moment it is not important to distinguish between these two sources of deviant behavior, except to point out that the severity of a "crime wave" cannot always be measured by the number of deviant offenders involved or the volume of deviance in fact committed. In the sense that the term is being used here, "crime wave" refers to a rash of publicity, a moment of excitement and alarm, a feeling that something needs to be done. It may or may not mean an actual increase in the volume of deviation.[1]

Second, the appearance of a boundary crisis does not necessarily mean that a *new* set of boundaries has attracted attention or even that some important change has taken place within the basic structure of the community itself. Ordinarily, it only means that a different sector of the community's traditional boundary network has moved into focus and needs to be more carefully

[1] The amount of publicity given to criminal activities, of course, does not usually tell us very much about the volume of crime actually committed. See F. James Davis, "Crime News in Colorado Newspapers," *American Journal of Sociology*, LVII (1952), pp. 325–330. Or see Lincoln Steffen's account of the day he personally started a "crime wave" in New York in his *Autobiography* (New York: Harcourt, Brace, and World, 1931).

defined. For instance, most citizens of the United States went into the Second World War very conscious of the line separating "democracy" from "fascism," since this distinction represented one of the critical baselines of the American way; but these same citizens emerged from the war into a world where the line separating "democracy" from "communism" had assumed a sudden prominence. This change of focus did not indicate the appearance of "new" boundaries, of course, but a shift of national attention from one established boundary sector to another, and the various investigations which followed during the McCarthy era can be understood to some extent as an attempt on the part of the larger community to become better informed about the nature and location of that line.

In the same way, the different crime waves which swept across the colony of Massachusetts Bay during the seventeenth century each followed a period of unsettling historical change, during which the boundaries which set the New England Way apart as a special kind of ethic threatened to become more obscure. Using this sketchy model as a guide, we will inquire in the present chapter why the New England saints became so alarmed by the heresy they called Antinomianism, why they treated the Quakers among them with such sudden violence, and why, finally, they began to fear that the air around them was alive with witches.

One final remark might be made before we turn to a discussion of the three crime waves. The narratives retold on these pages are not meant to amend or improve upon other accounts available in the historical literature. The Antinomian controversy and the witchcraft hysteria in particular have been the subject of excellent studies in recent years,[2] and the only reason for repeating the stories here is that the reader (not to mention the

[2] For the Antinomian crisis see Emery Battis, *Saints and Sectaries* (Chapel Hill, N.C.: University of North Carolina Press, 1962). For the witchcraft episode see Marion L. Starkey, *The Devil in Massachusetts* (New York: Knopf, 1949).

writer) needs to be caught up in the historical sweep of these events before their sociological significance becomes evident.

The Antinomian Controversy

The Antinomian controversy of 1636–1638 did not begin as a "crime wave" in any ordinary sense. It was a convulsive episode, a moment of restlessness which moved across the colony like a puff of wind and suddenly exploded into one of the stormiest events in a whole generation of New England history. If the men and women who provoked the crisis had been better organized and surer of their own purposes, we might remember them as founders of an important new social movement. But as it was, few of those active people really understood the significance of the theory they advanced or the violence of the storm they managed to stir up. Most of them thought they were engaged in a local argument about church affairs and continued to think so until the day they found themselves banished as criminals, disarmed as potential revolutionaries, or asked to recant crimes they had never known they were committing. In that respect, the shape of the Antinomian crisis only became apparent after it had been settled in the usual Puritan fashion—by a raw display of power.

In 1636, when the dispute first came to public attention, Massachusetts was in the midst of a vast building program. The flow of immigrants from England had reached a high peak and settlements were spreading across the hinterlands of Boston Bay and reaching far out into the wilderness. The settlers were surveying the dimensions of their new territory, not only in the sense that they were subdividing the land into separate freeholds, marking off areas of common pasturage, and laying out the ground plans of new towns, but also in the sense that they were drawing the outlines of their political and religious institutions. The "New England Way" was emerging from the fogs of Puritan theory and taking measured form in the maps of growing towns and in the diagrams of new government agencies.

The main purpose of the Puritan experiment in those early days was to show that men could govern themselves in a political state exactly as they governed themselves in a church congregation—that the Bible could serve as a competent instrument of law, that sainthood could provide a feasible basis for citizenship, and that the ministers could act as the final moral authority in civil as well as spiritual matters. As the commonwealth slowly took form, then, the Puritan magistrates began to operate on the basis of a political theory which borrowed most of its metaphors from English Congregationalism but which represented something of a departure from at least the mood of that earlier doctrine. In its first stages, as we have seen, Puritanism can be said to have contained a strong note of individualism, if only in the sense that it appealed directly to the individual conscience and promoted a respect for private religious expression and experience. Now this sense of individuality fit naturally into Puritan thinking so long as it was voiced by a people protesting against the authority of a Rome or a Canterbury, but when these protesters themselves moved into power and became the custodians of their own church, a rapid shift in emphasis was necessary. By virtue of one long sea voyage, the New England Puritans had been transformed from an opposition party into a ruling elite, and one of the central concerns for the Massachusetts leadership was to capture the emotional resources which had sustained the earlier protest and harness them to the needs of a tightly disciplined orthodoxy. Thus a new brand of Puritanism was taking shape in the forests of New England: the piety and self-expression which had dominated the original tone of the movement was gradually being transformed into the loyalty and obedience necessary for a civil establishment. A people who had trained themselves to police their own hearts and control their own impulses were now being asked to apply the same discipline to the community as a whole.

Whereas the early Puritan theorists had emphasized the

private nature of each person's covenant with God, the New England theorists began to argue that God had entered into a covenant with the people of the colony as a corporate group and was only ready to deal with them through the agencies they had built to govern themselves. Thus the key idea of the new theology was that an individual's relationship to God needed to be screened by some intermediate level of authority—a congregation, a government, an administration. Looking back at this shift in focus from the seasoned perspective of another century, it would seem that the people of the Bay were constructing much the same kind of control apparatus they had fought against in England; but some form of external discipline was necessary if the colony were to survive at all, and few settlers seemed concerned that the earlier individualism of the movement was quietly disappearing. In theory, at least, each soul was left to negotiate his own way to heaven and was encouraged to act upon the promptings of his own conscience; but in fact, an administrative machinery was slowly developing to make sure that each private conscience was rightly informed and loyal to the policies and programs of the state. The clergy, naturally, played an important role in this arrangement. It became their job to keep order among the various congregations, to instruct men in their duty toward the state as well as toward God, and perhaps most important, to lead the congregation in deciding what persons were eligible for membership in the larger corporation. Ministers could not hold public office, nor could they interfere too actively in political affairs, but they played a leading part in determining who among the settlers had experienced a true conversion and so deserved the privileges of the franchise. In many respects, the whole structure of the New England Way rested on that one article, for the purpose of the enterprise was to prove that God's chosen saints could and should take charge of His earthly commonwealth. No one would pretend that there were any infallible guidelines for deciding who was saved and who was not, but someone had to make human judgments in the absence of divine knowledge, and this responsibility, inevitably, fell to the clergy.

As we shall see, the Antinomian controversy centered on that very point, for it was the contention of Mrs. Hutchinson and her followers that almost no ministers in the Bay were competent to judge whether a person was truly touched by grace or not, and in doing so, they were challenging one of the most important cornerstones of the whole experiment. They were saying in effect that the spirited individualism of the old movement could not be converted into the orthodoxy of the new, and they did so at a time when this difference meant all the world to the settlers of New England.

The Antinomian controversy was probably the most momentous event which took place in the first decade of settlement, but it was often a confusing affair even to its most active participants. John Winthrop, in a passage to be quoted later, decided that few people really understood the issues at stake, and sixty years afterward Cotton Mather concluded: " 'Tis believed that multitudes of persons, who took in with both parties, did never to their dying hour understand what their difference was." [3] Yet Winthrop, Mather, and every subsequent historian of the period seem to agree that this crisis was one of the most serious moments in the early development of the Bay: somehow the incident defined New England Puritanism in the middle 1630's as no other event and no other theory could have, because it marked a shift of boundaries which the settlers of Massachusetts could not articulate in any other way.

I

The story of the controversy should properly begin with an introduction to its principal characters.

When John Winthrop died in 1649, he was the unquestioned

---

[3] Cotton Mather, *Magnalia Christi Americana, or The Ecclesiastical History of New-England* (Hartford, Conn.: Silas Andrus, 1853), I, p. 508. Cited hereafter as Mather, *Magnalia*.

leader of his people and in every respect entitled to be remembered as the founder of Massachusetts. But in the middle of the 1630's, Winthrop's popularity had suffered an abrupt decline both in the colony at large and in his home parish of Boston. In 1634 he had seen the crusty Thomas Dudley elected Governor in his place, and again the following year he had been overlooked in favor of John Haynes, a relative newcomer to the Bay. It is difficult to guess what lay underneath this unexpected shift of fortune. Perhaps the freemen were exercising their new voting strength in a warning to the magistrates; perhaps they were offended by the aristocratic position Winthrop had taken with respect to the code of law and several other issues which had come to public attention in the early years of the settlement. But whatever the reason, the Puritans had again duplicated Biblical history by turning away from their Moses.

In Boston, too, Winthrop's influence had begun to fade. He had been one of the charter members of the local church, active in all its affairs and closely associated with its two distinguished ministers—who were both to play prominent roles in the crisis. John Wilson was the preacher of the church, by all contemporary accounts an earnest, conventional, and somewhat irritable man. John Cotton, who shared the Boston pulpit with Wilson in the strange New England system of dual ministry, was one of the leading Puritan theorists of the English-speaking world and a man of immense prestige in the colony. Throughout the period before the Antinomian crisis, these three men had enjoyed a partnership patterned after the best Puritan traditions. Wilson ruled the Boston congregation with a loyal eye toward the needs of the magistracy, and Winthrop, in his turn, performed his duties as an elder in the church with a high sense of responsibility. Cotton played the part of Aaron to Winthrop's Moses, supporting him politically and on at least one occasion even taking to the stump for him during a popular election for the Governorship. By 1636, however, the three associates had been caught up in a peculiar set of currents. Wilson was beginning to sense that he had lost support among members of his own congregation, a decline in influence much like that experienced by Winthrop, and both Wilson and Winthrop were slowly becoming aware that even John Cotton was acting somewhat differently toward them.

While all of this was going on, an important new face appeared in Boston. Henry Vane was then a man of twenty-three, son of one of the most powerful men in England and a favorite of the King himself. Vane had not yet developed the qualities that were later to make him an outstanding political figure in the troubled years of Cromwell's reign, but he was an appealing personage to the people of the Bay and at once became a force in Massachusetts politics. He had a patrician's bearing and a quick, easy sympathy with the more advanced ideas of the day, yet at the same time he could be sentimental, indiscreet, and remarkably naive. Vane represented a new drift in Boston society. For one thing, he expressed his Puritan convictions with a grace and style that had an immediate impact on the hardened settlers of the Bay. But beyond this, Vane belonged to the contemporary world of Europe. There was a scope to his imagination, a grandness even in his mistakes, that seemed to demand a larger theater than Massachusetts could provide, and this quality was highly attractive to a people long isolated from their native land. At the time of the Antinomian controversy, then, Vane had just made a splendid entrance into Massachusetts and was beginning to take advantage of his huge popularity. In 1636, at the age of twenty-four, he was elected Governor, the third consecutive year in which John Winthrop had been left out of that office.

No sooner had Vane assumed his new duties than it began to be whispered that he had joined a faction in Boston which entertained some very peculiar opinions. One settler wrote to a friend in London: "Mr. Vane coming from England a young gentleman, was presently elected governor, and before he was half warm in his seat, to show his spirit, began to broach new tenets . . . [and] agitated with such violence as if they had been matters of that consequnce that the peace and welfare of New England must be sacrificed rather than they should not take place." [4]

Most of these opinions seemed to originate from a private home in Boston where William Hutchinson lived with his wife Anne. Mrs. Hutchinson was then in her middle forties, a woman of lively intelligence who loved to discuss the more obscure points of Puritan theology and who knew how to defend her opinions with a formidable display of Biblical scholarship. Although the Hutchinsons had only arrived in the colony a short time earlier, Anne's talent for stirring up discussion and provoking controversy was widely respected in Boston. It must be remembered that religious activities were almost the only entertainment known in the Bay, and since the Hutchinson home always rang with the sound of religious conversation, it soon became an important community center—a kind of theological salon. As many as eighty people might gather in the parlor to talk about the sermon of the last Sabbath, and in these discussions the most prominent voice almost always belonged to Mrs. Hutchinson herself. Winthrop thought her "a woman of haughty and fierce carriage, of a nimble wit and active spirit, and a very voluble tongue," [5] but visitors to her home might have added that she could debate a point of theology so compellingly that at times she seemed almost inspired. Before long, the household seminars in Mrs. Hutchinson's parlor were far more popular than the official sermons of John Wilson. Not only did most of the Boston congregation turn to her for religious counsel, but many of the ranking magistrates, including the young Governor, ap-

[4] Thomas Hutchinson, *The History of the Colony and Province of Massachusetts-Bay* . . . (Boston: Thomas and John Fleet, 1764 and 1767), I, pp. 64–65. Cited hereafter as Hutchinson, *History*.

[5] John Winthrop, "A Short Story of the Rise, Reign, and Ruin of Antinomians, Familists and Libertines, that Infected the Churches of New England," London, 1644, in *Antinomianism in the Colony of Massachusetts Bay, 1636–1638*, edited by Charles Francis Adams (Boston: Publications of the Prince Society, 1894), p. 138.

peared at her meetings regularly. "It was a wonder," Winthrop wrote sadly, "upon what a sudden the whole church of Boston (some few excepted) were become her converts." [6]

At first, the discussions in Mrs. Hutchinson's home seem to have been rather general in scope, but as excitement grew in Boston about the apparent revolt of Wilson's congregation the whole issue began to take on a more serious note. Perhaps, as Winthrop later claimed, there were only a few persons in Boston who really appreciated the finer points of Mrs. Hutchinson's argument, and perhaps she was not altogether sure herself; but there was one subject on which her opinion was quite clear to everyone. She felt that only two ministers in the commonwealth were familiar enough with what she called the "covenant of grace" to qualify for their jobs, and she took special pains to point out that John Wilson was not one of them. The terms in which these views were expressed do not matter for the moment, but it is important to say something about the two clergymen who were exempted from that harsh judgment. The first, John Cotton, has already been introduced. Mrs. Hutchinson had been acquainted with the teachings of this great man for some time, having been a follower of his in England and having migrated to the new world in order to remain under his ministry. In the entire controversy which followed, Mrs. Hutchinson rarely offered an opinion which she did not attribute to Cotton—a source of obvious embarrassment to him.

The second minister to escape this sweeping indictment was the Reverend John Wheelwright, a newcomer to the Bay. Wheelwright had landed in Boston only a few hours after Vane's election to the Governor's chair, and he seemed to celebrate his safe arrival by plunging immediately into the dispute. He was related to Mrs. Hutchinson by marriage, which may have spurred him into action a little sooner; but it is likely that he would have found his way into the battle zone even without that encourage-

[6] *Ibid.*, p. 161.

ment, for Wheelwright had been fired to a high pitch by the dissensions then raging in England, and, like many of his contemporaries at home, was in a sharp, contentious mood. In many ways, he represented a brand of Puritanism which would soon appear in the ranks of Cromwell's army but had not yet found expression among the narrower saints of the Bay. Massachusetts met several men of this stamp, persons whose theological leanings were slowly bringing them to the notion that states might tolerate a diversity of religious opinions: Henry Vane was one of them, Roger Williams another, and Wheelwright very clearly belongs in that company. It is a fitting footnote to Massachusetts history that all three of these men later achieved prominence in the work of the Great Rebellion and saw their ideas take root in the more receptive soil of England.

When Wheelwright arrived in Boston, then, long before the revolt began in England, he was already sensitive to the sounds of controversy; and it is entirely appropriate that his appearance on the scene should touch off the first serious skirmish between the admirers of Anne Hutchinson and the ruling cadre of the community.

The skirmish began when some members of the Boston congregation, presumably acting at Mrs. Hutchinson's suggestion, proposed that Wheelwright be taken into the church as an associate to Cotton. Wilson was understandably reluctant to accept the proposal, and the argument which followed showed in cruel detail how far he had been divided from his flock. Only four or five persons stood with him through the bitter exchange, but one of them was John Winthrop, and the neglected old leader seems to have risen to the occasion with unusual force and determination. According to the rules of congregational assembly then in effect, no resolution could be passed by the church unless some kind of working consensus was reached, and as a result of Winthrop's outspoken objections the issue was silently (if sullenly) dropped. Wheelwright accepted a call to another congregation; for the moment, at least, open conflict had been postponed.

But the brief scrimmage had brought about two lasting effects. First, it indicated clearly how the opposing sides would line up in the event of further trouble: Mrs. Hutchinson could gather almost the entire congregation to her defense, while Wilson was left in a painfully insecure position, weakened on the one flank by the fading prestige of Winthrop and exposed on the other by the apparent neutrality of Cotton. Second, the quarrel had been loud enough to draw notice from other parts of the colony and soon the odd disturbances in Boston were a topic of conversation everywhere.

The New England Puritans had great confidence in their own powers of reason and generally responded to moments of crisis by calling meetings to discuss the matter; and so, like many another disagreement in the history of the Bay, the Antinomian controversy opened with a series of conferences. Ministers from every corner of the country arrived in Boston to consider the problems of the local church, consulting with Winthrop, arguing with Vane, pleading with Cotton, and at least once confronting Mrs. Hutchinson herself. To a man, the visiting clergy were sympathetic to John Wilson, and before the conference season had run its normal course almost every temper in Boston had been drawn to a fine edge. On one occasion, Governor Vane opened a meeting of the magistrates by breaking into tears and threatening to leave the colony altogether, an indiscretion which he later reconsidered when pressed by the people of Boston. On another occasion, Wilson stood before a gathering of the colony's leading men and delivered a slashing attack on the Boston church, for which he was almost censured by his own congregation. And finally, as if to seal the disaster, Mrs. Hutchinson met with a delegation of ministers and announced that none of them were competent to preach the gospel. Faced by this alarm-

ing situation, the visiting clergy shortly abandoned their mission
of peace and began to operate as a fact-finding commission:
Massachusetts was beginning to prepare its case against the Boston insurgents.

While these events were taking place, the people of Boston
became more and more restless. Tired of challenging Wilson in
his own pulpit, they began to travel around the countryside in
spirited groups, heckling other ministers, disturbing other congregations, until the air of Massachusetts was charged with excitement. Winthrop reported:

Thus every occasion increased the contention, and caused great alienation of minds; and the members of Boston (frequenting the lectures
of other ministers) did make much disturbance by public questions,
and objections to their doctrines, which did any way disagree from
their opinions; and so it began to be as common here to distinguish
between men, by being under a covenant of grace or a covenant of
works, as in other countries between Protestants and papists.[7]

As the conference season drew to a close, then, conservative elements in the country were thoroughly aroused and ready
to fight, but it was evident that many people were not really
sure what the fighting would be about. It was Winthrop's opinion that "except men of good understanding, and such as knew
the bottom of the tenets of those of the other party, few could
see where the difference was," [8] nor does the situation seem much
clearer three hundred years later. Somehow a battle would be
fought over issues which had not yet earned a name—issues important enough to bring men to blows but not well enough defined to permit articulate discussion.

Mrs. Hutchinson's debate with the ministry of Massachusetts was conducted in such an exhausting barrage of words and

[7] Winthrop, Journal, I, p. 219.
[8] Winthrop, Journal, I, pp. 216–217.

ideas that the underlying shape of the quarrel is difficult to follow—particularly if we are encouraged by the tone of the argument to assume that it was theological rather than political. The
historian Charles Francis Adams concluded:

Not only were the points in dispute obscure, but the discussion was
carried on in a jargon which has become unintelligible; and, from a
theological point of view, it is now devoid of interest. At most, it can
excite only a faint curiosity as one more example of the childish excitement over trifles by which people everywhere and at all times
are liable to be swept away from the moorings of common sense.[9]

Adam's exasperation with the text of the debate must be
taken seriously, for no student has ever studied the episode more
carefully. Still, the importance of the Antinomian controversy
lies not so much in what was said as in the form of the events
which followed. In order to understand why sensible people
would brawl over such "trifles" we should look at the larger situation rather than the details of the argument itself, for the affair had a shape and a logic which were not wholly reflected in
the words that were spoken.

To begin with, Mrs. Hutchinson was a woman, and this
simple matter must have added appreciably to the elders' sense
of irritation. Puritan notions about the role of women in community life were less than progressive even by the standards of
the seventeenth century—a fact made abundantly clear by Winthrop when he explained that a woman of his acquaintance had
become mentally ill as a result of reading too many books: "for,"
he added by way of editorial, "if she had attended her household affairs, and such things as belong to women, and not gone
out of her way and calling to meddle in such things as are proper
for men, she had kept her wits, and might have improved them
usefully and honorably in the place that God had set her." [10]
Needless to say, men like Winthrop would have been annoyed

9 Charles Francis Adams, *Three Episodes*, I, p. 367.
10 Winthrop, Journal, II, p. 225.

by a woman of Mrs. Hutchinson's belligerent intelligence whether they knew what she was talking about or not.

In one respect, however, everyone knew what Mrs. Hutchinson was talking about. When she declared that only Cotton and Wheelwright among the many ministers of the Bay were "walking in a covenant of grace," with the obvious corollary that the others all preached a "covenant of works," she was touching a highly sensitive nerve in her Puritan audience. Vague as they were, these two phrases had played a prominent role in the early history of the Reformation and were still capable of stirring up old angers and insecurities.

According to the Puritan reading of Genesis, God had once promised Adam that his seed would enjoy everlasting life so long as he kept away from the tree of knowledge, the forbidden fruit. Adam had failed to honor that straightforward contract, of course, and mankind had been condemned to toil, hardship, and eventual death. But then God offered another covenant to man in which He agreed to save a scattering of persons from damnation in an entirely arbitrary way, drawing them at random from among His people and bestowing His grace upon them in advance. The most important feature of this new covenant was that there would be no more guarantees, no more opportunities for men to earn salvation by a display of good conduct. At its simplest, the first of these arrangements was the covenant of works, while the latter substitute was the covenant of grace.

Now these two "covenants" were essentially an invention of Reformation thinking. When the first generation of reformers challenged the authority of Rome, they argued that the formal structure of the Catholic Church—its regulations, its formulae, its alms and dispensations—were really a throwback to the forfeited covenant of works, because the Church seemed to be teaching that men could earn their way to heaven by observing a few simple rules exactly as Adam might have won salvation for all his seed by observing a single prohibition. The covenant of grace, then, had a very special meaning in this context. If salvation occurs at random and has no relation to the actual conduct of men on earth, then people do not need any religious services to prepare them for eternity or any class of priests to intercede in their behalf. Grace is an intimate exchange, a personal communication between God and His chosen saints.

Like many other tenets of Reformation thought, however, this distinction between grace and works was more often taken as a metaphor than as a literal sanction, one which might be interpreted literally by a sect struggling against an established church, but one which had to be phrased with extreme care by any party in power. In its purest form, the covenant of grace was almost an invitation to anarchy, for it encouraged people to be guided by an inner sense of urgency rather than by an outer form of discipline; if the notion were taken at face value there would be no end to the amount of mischief a person might do. Supposed someone mistook an upset stomach for a divine call and charged off to do battle with even the most legitimate authority? No, the covenant of grace might make good material for a revolutionary slogan, but it was hardly the kind of doctrine a government could afford to tolerate in its undiluted form once that government came to power. When Martin Luther first rebelled against Rome, for example, and broke his monastic vows, he justified his action on the ground that he had received a divine summons; but later, when all Germany was torn by the new doctrines and the peasants rose in what they thought was a religious crusade, he had to turn away in horror. Somehow the voices which spurred the peasants into civil war did not seem to have the same divinity as the voices which drew Luther away from the Church, and the problem for the more responsible reformers was to create an agency which could distinguish between the two without returning to the formality and discipline of the Catholic Church. Throughout the early history of the Reformation this dilemma had appeared again and again, and the people of New England were no more immune. They had confronted the Anglican bishops by arguing that each man should be free to negotiate his way to heaven without interference from a central church hierarchy, but now, with a land to settle and a people to govern, the tone of their argument was bound to change. When the Boston insurgents were called "Antinomians," the familiar cycle seemed to be repeating itself, for this was the name given to the desperate heretics of Luther's day and a name many ministers in the Bay had heard applied to themselves in old England.

Anne Hutchinson may not have been an Antinomian in the purest sense of the term, but she seemed to advocate a kind of religious enthusiasm which was simply not possible among an orthodox company of saints. She spoke to a people whose sense of theology had been sharpened by the endless controversies of the Reformation, and to them the main text of her argument was altogether clear. If saints are joined to God by a covenant of grace, she asked, why is it necessary for them to accept the discipline of an earthly church? If God bestows His grace directly on the recipient in a private moment of conversion, why should that gift be ratified by an official of the church who himself may not be chosen? It is difficult to know how far Mrs. Hutchinson meant to go in her distrust of church control, since few of her own words have survived. But she did announce that the incumbent ministers of the Bay were not fit to occupy their pulpits; and whatever else she might have thought about the role of church discipline in a community of saints, this opinion was quite enough to set the whole machinery of the state against her.

In several respects, then, Mrs. Hutchinson was only repeating an exaggerated version of what many Puritan preachers had said before, and perhaps it is true, as she claimed, that many of her ideas were drawn from the early sermons of John Cotton. But Puritan theory had been revised considerably since Cotton was a young minister in Lincolnshire. The credo of a minority group had become the platform of a ruling party, and in the process it had acquired a number of new responsibilities. Gradually, then, two amendments to the original theory of grace had worked their way into Congregational thinking, each of them representing a change in tone rather than a distinct change in doctrine. The first of these was the notion that certified ministers were competent to judge who had experienced a true conversion and who had not, giving them whatever warrant they needed to screen candidates for church membership and for the franchise. The second was the notion that even the surest saint should be subject to church discipline and governed by the will of the congregation, not because his future reward depended upon it, exactly, but because a person needs to be adequately prepared for the gift of grace when it comes. The ministers were careful to point out that these shifts in theory did not represent any return to the discredited covenant of works, but the line between the two positions became more and more difficult to see as it became apparent that one of the easiest ways for a person to convince his fellows that he was truly saved was to become a devoted servant of the church and a loyal citizen of the state. As Mrs. Hutchinson very correctly sensed, a new strain had appeared in New England thinking. The ministers were not arguing that outer conformity was necessary to *earn* salvation, but they seemed to be saying that outer conformity was a convenient way to *prove* salvation; and thus the covenant of grace had lost so much of its inner mystery that it did bear some resemblance to the older covenant of works. The clergy were quite positive that they could explain the difference logically, but they spent so many awkward hours in this pursuit that they appeared to betray their uneasiness every time they mounted the pulpit or took their pens in hand.

The danger of Mrs. Hutchinson's position, of course, was that she did not want to give the ministers the authority they needed to use the covenant of grace as a political instrument. In the beginning, perhaps, her quarrel with the clergy was a personal matter: she was entirely confident of her own election and did not think for a moment that a preacher like Wilson, whatever his offices or degrees from Cambridge, was competent to review her qualifications for sainthood. She was quite sure that godly behavior on this earth was no evidence that one had been chosen for salvation in the next. Now all of this was according to the best Puritan usage of a generation earlier, and had she addressed her arguments to the Anglican churchmen rather than the New England divines, she might have earned a good deal of credit for her stand. But Mrs. Hutchinson did not appreciate how the world had changed. Sainthood in New England had become a political responsibility as well as a spiritual condition, and when she hinted that her election set her above the government of ordinary men she seemed to be asking for a license which no administration could safely confer. It is important to remember that Mrs. Hutchinson did not really ask for such a license, nor did she deny the jurisdiction of the government over her—but she had chosen a highly suggestive metaphor in an attempt to phrase her discontents accurately, and in doing so, had reminded these children of the Reformation about issues that had been festering under the surface for many years. It was not Mrs. Hutchinson's voice so much as her echo which started the Antinomian controversy in Massachusetts Bay.

The case against Mrs. Hutchinson and her followers, then, was largely a political one. The arguments which emerged from the Hutchinson parlor were cloaked in the language of theology, but (to the extent that the two could be distinguished in seventeenth-century thought) the charge against them was sedition rather than heresy, and once the leading men of the colony began to notice the effect Mrs. Hutchinson's crusade was producing among the settlers of the Bay, they moved heavily to the attack.

By the end of 1636, the magistrates were ready to prosecute their case against the Boston insurgents. They could not afford to mount their offensive with a massive show of force, since the

Boston contingent was by now very strong, but they began to chip away at the roots of that strength in a methodical, systematic way.

The first blow was struck rather hesitantly. Late in 1636, Wheelwright had given a lecture in Boston at the invitation of the local congregation, and now, in the early days of 1637, the Court of Assistants called him before the bench on a charge of inciting sedition. The lecture which provoked this action is one of the most interesting exhibits to have survived from the time: like so many of the salvos exchanged during the controversy, the text of Wheelwright's sermon is extremely difficult to follow, but it contains a note of anger—a hint, even, of violence—which can still be sensed three centuries later.

The way we must take, if so be we will not have the Lord Jesus Christ taken from us, is this, we must all prepare for a spiritual combat, we must put on the whole armor of God . . . and we must have our loins girt and be ready to fight. . . . We must all of us prepare for battle and come out against the enemies of the Lord and if we do not strive, those under a covenant of works will prevail.[11]

Wheelwright's trial began behind closed doors and lasted several days. In the end he was found guilty of contempt and sedition, but the decision had been so close and popular reaction so strong that the court postponed sentence until a later and calmer date. Wheelwright was not an important target for the magistrates anyway, and they were willing to bide their time until a more serious problem could be disposed of.

That problem was Governor Vane. Although his enormous popularity had faded somewhat in the colony as a whole, Vane was still the champion of Boston and a symbol of great importance to the Antinomian cause. Yet his increasing identification with the Boston faction had indirectly brought about a realignment of political forces throughout the whole of the colony. If

[11] John Wheelwright, *Papers,* edited by Charles H. Bell (Boston: Publications of the Prince Society, 1876), pp. 160–161.

nothing else, the early skirmishes had acted to dust off the firing line, and now that the outlines of the dispute were more clearly defined, the rest of the settlers began to sort themselves on either side of that line in preparation for the coming conflict. In the course of this realignment, John Winthrop emerged from retirement to take charge of the conservative forces; and thus the two rivals, so alike in stature but so different in temperament, became the leading candidates for the election of 1637. The magistrates had prepared a friendly ground for Winthrop's return to power by moving the election site from Boston to Cambridge (an imposing distance in those days) and the conservative party took every advantage of the situation. Not only did Winthrop win back the Governorship by an impressive margin, but Vane and two other leaders of the Boston group were left out of the magistracy altogether, a telling rebuke from people who ordinarily looked upon public office as the prerogative of rank.

This shift of fortune changed the complexion of the controversy entirely. Every magistrate in the country was soon opposed to the Hutchinson faction and all but two or three of the elected Deputies; but even with this huge arsenal of weapons the prosecution continued to press its case cautiously. In May of 1637, the General Court issued an order that no stranger could remain in the colony longer than three weeks without the express permission of one of the magistrates,[12] an act deliberately passed to seal the Boston group off from reinforcements, "for it was very probable," Winthrop tells us candidly, "that they expected many of their opinion to come out of England." [13] This action brought the level of excitement in the colony to a new pitch, and in the months that followed, a series of episodes occurred which added appreciably to the irritation of those already exposed nerves. To begin with, Winthrop carried out the full threat of the alien law by refusing permision for a group of new-

[12] Massachusetts Records, I, p. 196.
[13] Winthrop, Journal, I, p. 219.

comers to remain in the Bay, and this abrupt act, coming as it did from a man of known hospitality, contributed a new bitterness to the strain. Not long afterward a contingent of men from Boston refused to report for military service because their chaplain "walked in a covenant of works"—and this despite the fact that the colony was then engaged in a desperate war against the Pequot Indians. Meanwhile Vane sulked around Boston and on several occasions was pointlessly rude to Winthrop. And when these expressions of bad feeling had reached a crisis point, Vane suddenly set sail for England, leaving the Boston party without any political leadership at all.

Yet the magistrates were still hesitant to act, for despite the fact that they knew who the culprits were and what should be done with them, they did not know how to designate the crimes that had been committed. Men like John Wilson or Thomas Dudley could produce a marvelous stream of adjectives when called upon to describe the faults of Mrs. Hutchinson and her noisy followers, but for all their force and color these expressions did not constitute any kind of legal charge, even by the generous standards of Puritan justice. And so a religious synod was called in the summer of 1637 to clarify the matter. The ministers who traveled to Boston for this important convention were asked to provide the court with a base-line against which to judge the actions of the Antinomian group, to draw an explicit code of ecclesiastical law. Both Cotton and Wheelwright were invited to attend the meetings, as were all other ministers in the Bay, but the former seems to have been in a rather conciliatory mood and the latter seems to have been so shocked by the proceedings that he sat back and said very little. Before the synod ended, the clergy had engaged in a true orgy of heresy-hunting: they identified no less than eighty-two "unsafe opinions" before their spiritual appetites were satisfied and capped off that performance by adding nine "unwholesome expressions" to the list. The convention lasted twenty-four days, during which time the roster of potential heresies was drawn to epic length and the magistrates were given the prosecution weapon they most urgently needed—an explicit outline of the orthodoxy they were about to defend. In the end, John Cotton, who must have been very exhausted by then, announced that he had seen the error of his ways.

Reinforced by the clear-cut sanction of the synod and relieved to find a hint of reconciliation in the attitude of John Cotton, the magistrates returned to their unfinished business with new vigor. They began by reaching deep into the files of the court for a document which had been all but forgotten. When Wheelwright had first been arrested for sedition the people of Boston had sent a petition to the court protesting the action, and now, a full eight months later, the petition was drawn out of obscurity to pad the case against the Boston insurgents. Winthrop cheerfully admitted that the court's new interest in the petition was little more than a pretext:

There was great hope that the late general assembly would have had some good effect in pacifying the troubles and dissensions about matters of religion; but it fell out otherwise. . . . Whereupon the general court, being assembled (on the second of November) and finding, upon consultation, that two so opposite parties could not contain in the same body, without apparent hazard of ruin to the whole, agreed to send away some of the principle; and for this a fair opportunity was offered by the remonstrance or petition, which they preferred to the court (on the ninth of March), wherein they affirm Mr. Wheelwright to be innocent, and that the court had contemned the truth of Christ, with divers other scandalous and seditious speeches.[14]

Taking measure of this "fair opportunity," the General Court fairly burst into action. In a rapid series of orders the court (1) dismissed two Deputies from Boston who had signed the petition, (2) banished the Reverend Wheelwright and Mrs. Hutchinson from the colony, (3) disfranchised eight other persons from Boston who had been among the offending faction, and (4)

[14] Winthrop, Journal, I, pp. 239–240.

rounded out the purge by disarming seventy-five persons in the country, including fifty-eight from Boston alone.

> Whereas the opinions and revelations of Mr. Wheelwright and Mrs. Hutchinson have seduced and led into dangerous errors many of the people here in New England, insomuch as there is just cause of suspicion that they, as others in Germany, in former times, may, upon some revelation, make some sudden eruption upon those that differ from them in judgment, for prevention whereof it is ordered, that all those whose names are underwritten shall (upon warning given or left at their dwelling houses) before the 30th of this month of November, deliver at Mr. Cane's house at Boston, all such guns, pistols, swords, powder, shot, and match as they shall be owners of, or have in their custody, upon pain of ten pounds for every default. . . .[15]

It was all over in a matter of days.

II

The civil trial of Anne Hutchinson took place in November, 1637, and a transcript of these proceedings has been preserved.[16] In many respects, the trial can tell us as much about the confusions generated by the Antinomian controversy as any number of other documents, for it is our only opportunity to see the opposing forces in actual confrontation. Although a lone woman stood before the bar, in poor health and entirely without counsel, a whole way of life was on trial. Anne Hutchinson represented not only a dissatisfied group of colonists numbering over a hundred but a strain of Puritanism which the colony could no longer afford to recognize. When Governor Winthrop and Mistress Hutchinson faced each other across the bare wooden table which served as a bench, they wore the expressions of an austere magistrate and of a brash, contentious housewife; but the voices in which they spoke carried a tone of far greater

---

[15] Massachusetts Records, I, pp. 211–212.
[16] Hutchinson, *History*, Appendix II, Vol. II, pp. 482–520.

significance. Mrs. Hutchinson symbolized the lively enthusiasm of the old Puritanism while Governor Winthrop symbolized the political maturity of the new, and the dialogue which followed can hardly be appreciated unless this is kept in mind. From its opening moments, the exchange seems restless and uncertain—which should not be at all surprising, for the two principals were trying to speak a language which had not yet been invented, to argue an issue which had not yet been defined. In a sense, the trial was an attempt to develop such a language.

The examination began with Winthrop taking the combined role of prosecutor and judge, a proper procedure in those days. Not once in his opening remarks did he mention any specific charges against the defendant, confining himself to terms like these: "Mrs. Hutchinson, you are called here as one of those that have troubled the peace of the commonwealth and the churches here. . . ."

MRS. HUTCHINSON: I am called here to answer before you but I hear no things laid to my charge.

GOV. WINTHROP: I have told you some already and more I can tell you.

MRS. HUTCHINSON: Name one, sir.

GOV. WINTHROP: Have I not named some already?

MRS. HUTCHINSON: What have I said or done?

GOV. WINTHROP: Why, for your doings, this you did: harbor and countenance those that are parties in this faction that you have heard of. . . .

MRS. HUTCHINSON: What law do they transgress?

GOV. WINTHROP: The law of God and of the state.

MRS. HUTCHINSON: In what particular?

GOV. WINTHROP: Why in this among the rest, whereas the Lord doth say honor thy mother and father. . . . This honor you have broken in countenancing them.

This weary exchange continued for some moments to no one's advantage until Winthrop abruptly cut it off with this ex-clamation: "We do not mean to discourse with those of your sex, but only this: you do adhere unto them and do endeavor to set forward this faction and so you do dishonor us."

A new line of inquiry was then introduced. Winthrop asked the defendant to cite a Biblical rule giving her the right to hold meetings in her house, and she answered smartly, "there lies a clear rule in Titus that the elder women should instruct the young"—but this evidence of scholarship made little impression on the court. Then Mrs. Hutchinson quite properly argued that the court should find rules to support its proceedings, rather than requiring her to defend her own, and this odd conversation ensued:

MRS. HUTCHINSON: I desire that you would then set me a rule by which I may put them away that come unto me and so have peace in the doing.

GOV. WINTHROP: You must show your rule to receive them.

MRS. HUTCHINSON: I have done it.

GOV. WINTHROP: I deny it, because I have brought more arguments than you have.

Thus the first round of the hearing ended on a note of sheer petulance. Here was the highest executive officer in the land quibbling with one of its most desperate heretics as if the whole affair were no more than a schoolyard dispute, yet the discomfort of Winthrop's position was certainly real: the state had no formal charges to bring against Mrs. Hutchinson other than an earnest conviction that something had to be done, and one of Winthrop's tasks in the early stages of the trial was to find some basis for an indictment. It was at this point that Thomas Dudley broke into the conversation to state the case for the prosecution in his rough, straightforward way.

I would go a little higher with Mrs. Hutchinson. About three years ago we were all in peace. Mrs. Hutchinson from that time she came hath made a disturbance, and some that came over with her in the ship did inform me what she was as soon as she landed. I being then in place dealt with the pastor and teacher of Boston and desired them to inquire of her, and then I was satisfied that she held nothing different from us. But within half a year after, she had vented divers of her strange opinions and had made parties in the country, and at length it comes that Mr. Cotton and Mr. Vane were of her judgment, but Mr. Cotton hath cleared himself that he was not of that mind. But now it appears by this woman's meetings that Mrs. Hutchinson has so forestalled the minds of many in the country by their resort to her meetings that she now hath a potent party in the country. Now if all these things have endangered us as from the foundation, and if she in particular hath disparaged all our ministers in the land . . . why, this is not to be suffered! And therefore being driven to the foundation [and] it being found that Mrs. Hutchinson is she that hath disparaged all the ministers and hath been the cause of what is fallen out, why we must take away the foundation and the building will fall.

At no time during the trial was the case put more directly or more honestly. Mrs. Hutchinson had become the leader of "a potent party in the country" and had "disparaged all our ministers," it was as simple as that; but Dudley's flat conclusion that "this is not to be suffered" could hardly be regarded a valid grounds for conviction. And so the spectacle continued.

During the early rounds of the hearing a number of ministers had been in the courtroom, and now they urged the magistrates to turn to a subject of special interest to them. The Reverend Hugh Peters, an irascible man even in his better moods, complained that the court had not yet considered the most important charge against Mrs. Hutchinson: her disrespect for the New England priesthood. One after another, the assembled ministers talked about the indignities they had suffered at the hands of the defendant, each of them recalling the famous meeting in Boston where she had questioned their competence. Peters' testimony was short and to the point:

Briefly, she told me that there was a wide and broad difference between our brother Mr. Cotton and ourselves. I desired to know the difference. She answered that he preaches the covenant of grace and you the covenant of works and that you are not able ministers of the New Testament and know no more than the apostles did before the resurrection of Christ. I then did put to her, what do you conceive of such a brother? She answered he had not the seal of the spirit.

Mrs. Hutchinson made some attempt to protect herself against this testimony of the ministers, but there was little she could do: she protested one or two minor inaccuracies, interrupted to argue about a small matter of phrasing, and dealt almost entirely with technicalities. It was almost as if she did not quite understand what was happening, for she seemed content to pick tiny details out of this torrent of evidence as it poured by her into the room and never once challenged the main substance of the testimony itself. The trial was left in this uncertain state when the court recessed for the day.

The next morning, refreshed, Mrs. Hutchinson opened the day's hearings by making an incredible request. She pointed out that the ministers were acting as prosecution witnesses rather than neutral spectators and asked that they repeat their testimony under oath. From a purely legal point of view, to be sure, her request was quite proper; but she had offered an outrageous affront to the ministers of the Bay. No matter how partisan their leanings, the clergy were still the spiritual authority of Christendom, and no one had ever proposed before that their word would have more credit if it were backed by a sworn oath. Both ministers and magistrates were thrown off balance by this odd turn of events and tempers grew quite short. On one occasion Dudley turned to an unfortunate colleague and asked, "what do you mean to trouble the court with such questions," and a few moments later the voice of John Endicott could be heard snapping at one of the Deputies, "I will tell you what I say, I think that this carriage of yours tends to further casting dirt upon the face of the judges." And Hugh Peters, who was not even a member of the court, took aim at one of the few defense witnesses and virtually commanded him to silence with a curt "how dare you look into the court to say such a thing." The elders were not yet ready to hear any defense testimony; they had not even decided what the prosecution case would be.

At this point John Cotton took the stand, and we may imagine that a hush spread quickly over the courtroom. This was one witness Peters could not silence with a sharp word of rebuke. Cotton had been present at the first meeting between Mrs. Hutchinson and the clergy, acting more or less as a friendly moderator, and now he was asked if his memory of the occasion coincided with that of his fellow ministers. His answer was careful almost to the point of equivocation, but after a time it became clear that Cotton did not "remember" the meeting as Peters and the others had reported it. "And I must say," he added, "that I did not find her saying that they were under a covenant of works, nor that she said they did preach a covenant of works." This was an extremely serious problem to the court, for the prosecution could not easily proceed without more help from this eminent man.

It was Anne Hutchinson herself who came to the court's rescue. Perhaps she wanted to take advantage of the momentary confusion; perhaps her high sense of theater got the better of her. Or perhaps deviants of her kind are compelled by some inner urgings to make a "profession" of feelings which their judges can only receive as a "confession," but whatever the reason she suddenly launched into a long account of her own life and ended the recital by declaring that her insights were a result of direct revelation. "I bless the Lord, He hath let me see which was the clear ministry and which the wrong." Even after all these years, one can sense the excitement which slowly took hold of the judges as they began to understand what was happening.

MR. NOWELL: How did you know that this was the spirit?

MRS. HUTCHINSON: How did Abraham know that it was God did bid him to offer his son, it being a breach of the sixth commandment?

DEP. GOV. DUDLEY: By an immediate voice.

MRS. HUTCHINSON: So to me by an immediate voice.

DEP. GOV. DUDLEY: How? An immediate revelation?

MRS. HUTCHINSON: By the voice of His own spirit to my soul.

In the growing fever of the moment Mrs. Hutchinson continued to add to her fateful performance. The Lord revealed Himself to her regularly, she confided, and she fully expected to be delivered from the judgment of the court as Daniel had been delivered from the lion's den. Moreover she warned the court that "if you go on in this course you will bring a curse upon you and your posterity, and the mouth of the Lord hath spoken it."

Whether she knew it or not, Anne Hutchinson had given her judges the charge they had sought so energetically, for no item stood higher on the Puritan list of heresies than the claim that God revealed Himself directly to men. True, God had spoken directly to Abraham and had even commanded him to commit a terrible crime, but that was before the law of God had been published in its final form, and besides, no sensible person believed that God would let His will be known to individual men when so excellent an instrument as the church was available for that purpose. Every respected minister in Christendom agreed on at least this one point, that the age of revelation was over. Mrs. Hutchinson had used a very poor example in her speech to the magistrates, for (as so often happens in cases of this sort) she was realizing their worst fears before their very eyes. She was saying that her communion with God yielded revelations "as true as the Scriptures" and gave her full sanction to operate outside the law.

At this point the court turned to poor John Cotton and asked if he had any further comments to make in Mrs. Hutchinson's behalf. Cotton hedged as neatly as he could, offering a learned lecture on the subject of revelation, but he did not have his usual command of the audience and in the middle of his discourse Dudley spoke to him in a manner quite new to his experience: "Sir, you weary me and do not satisfy me." In the end Cotton had no choice but to step aside, and as he did a tidal wave of judgment crashed around Mrs. Hutchinson. Even the normally gentle Winthrop could not resist a cry of triumph:

I see a marvellous providence of God to bring things to this pass. . . . Now the mercy of God by a providence hath answered our desires and made her to lay open herself and the ground of all these disturbances to be by revelations . . . for this is the thing that hath been the root of all the trouble . . . Aye, it is the most desperate enthusiasm in the world.

And then the whole court began to take up the chant.

MR. NOWELL: I think it is a devilish delusion.

GOV. WINTHROP: Of all the revelations that ever I read of I never read the like ground laid for this. . . .

DEP. GOV. DUDLEY: I never saw such revelations as these among the Anabaptists. . . . These disturbances that have come among the Germans have all been grounded upon revelations, and so they that have vented them have stirred up their hearers to take arms against their prince and to cut the throats of one another, and these have been the fruit of them, and whether the devil may inspire the same into their hearts here I know not, [but] I am fully persuaded that Mrs. Hutchinson is deluded by the devil, because the spirit of God speaks truth in all his servants.

GOV. WINTHROP: I am persuaded that the revelation she brings forth is delusion. (At this point the trial record notes: "all but two or three ministers cry out 'we all believe it, we all believe it.'")

MR. BROWN: . . . I think she deserves no less a censure than hath been already past but rather something more, for this is the foundation of all mischief and of all bastardly things. . . .

The rest was formality. The court had its charge, the defense had withdrawn, and now only a few procedural details remained. A discussion then took place about the defendant's notion that the clergy be sworn (a subject so boring to Dudley that he pouted "we shall all be sick with fasting") and it was determined that the ministers should be given the oath. They repeated their testimony and that was that. It was Winthrop who polled the court and announced its decision to Mrs. Hutchinson.

GOV. WINTHROP: The court hath already declared themselves satisfied concerning the things you hear, and concerning the troublesomeness of her spirit and the danger of her course among us, which is not to be suffered. Therefore if it be the mind of the court that Mrs. Hutchinson is unfit for our society, and if it be the mind of the court that she shall be banished out of our liberties and imprisoned till she be sent away, let them hold up their hands.

(All but three)

GOV. WINTHROP: Those that are contrary minded hold up yours.

(Mr. Coddington and Mr. Colburn only)

MR. HENNISON: I cannot hold up my hand one way or the other, and I will give my reason if the court require it.

GOV. WINTHROP: Mrs. Hutchinson, the sentence of the court you hear is that you are banished from out our jurisdiction as being a woman not fit for our society, and are to be imprisoned till the court shall send you away.

MRS. HUTCHINSON: I desire to know wherefore I am banished.

GOV. WINTHROP: Say no more, the court knows wherefore and is satisfied.

Modern readers often find it difficult to read the transcript of Anne Hutchinson's trial without projecting their twentieth-century sympathies into that seventeenth-century text. The proceedings were surely a cruel miscarriage of justice, even by the standards of the time, and it seems entirely natural to cast the poor defendant in a martyr's role. But this may be a misleading way to see the story, for Mrs. Hutchinson was a full partner in the transactions which led to her banishment and did as much as anyone else to set its basic tone and character. We do not know whether she got what she *wanted* from the court, of course, but it is fairly clear that she got what she *expected*, and in fact played an active role in realizing that prediction. Both sides tried to goad the other into making a declaration of their position; both hoped to establish the line which distinguished Mrs. Hutchinson's brand of Congregationalism from the more orthodox stand of the magistrates.

On the whole, then, it is easier to understand the main drift of the hearing if one forgets for the moment that it took the form of a criminal trial. The confrontation between Anne Hutchinson and the magistrates of Massachusetts was a tribal ceremony, a morality play, a ritual encounter between two traditional adversaries, and it is fair to assume that both the prosecution and the defense were more aware of the informal rules governing the occasion than any of the commentators who have studied it since. Like dancers tracing the steps of a familiar ceremony, all the participants in the drama must have known what its eventual outcome would be; but the form of the ritual had to be observed if that outcome were to have any lasting meaning. Although the trial continued for many hours, through many shifts of topic and many changes of legal posture, it never lost its relentless tone of certainty. In the end, Winthrop invited the court's verdict with almost the same phrase used by Dudley at the beginning of the proceedings: "The court hath already declared themselves satisfied concerning the things you hear, and concerning the troublesomeness of her spirit and the danger of her course among us, which is not to be suffered." And a moment later, when Mrs. Hutchinson asked the court to explain the basis of its decision, she was told flatly, "say no more, the court knows wherefore and is satisfied."

And that was exactly the point. The court *did* know why Mrs. Hutchinson had to be banished, but it did not know how to express that feeling in any language then known in New England. The settlers were experiencing a shift in ideological focus, a change in community boundaries, but they had no vocabulary to explain to themselves or anyone else what the nature of these changes were. The purpose of the trial was to invent that language, to find a name for the nameless offense which Mrs. Hutchinson had committed. All in all, Anne Hutchinson and her band of followers were guilty of something called "Hutchinsonianism," no more and no less, and one of the main outcomes of the trial

was to declare in no uncertain terms that people who acted in
this fashion had trespassed the revised boundaries of the New
England Way.

Massachusetts was not yet through with Mrs. Hutchinson.
After the trial she was kept for four months at the home of one
of the leading men in the colony and in March, 1638, was released
from confinement to undergo another examination, this time before the Boston congregation. The state had taken care of her
temporal fate by sentencing her to banishment, and now it was
time for the church to deal with her spiritual condition. During
the interval between the two trials, however, a number of changes
had taken place in the political climate of the Bay. Most important, John Cotton had completely gone over to the conservative
camp and had worked with great energy to bring the Boston
insurgents back into line. He began to complain that he had been
the "stalking horse" of the Antinomian faction and had never
been a party to the peculiar opinions of Mrs. Hutchinson.[17] Winthrop reports with understandable relish that Cotton "did spend
most of his time, both publicly and privately, to discover those
errors, and to reduce such as were gone astray." [18] When Mrs.
Hutchinson returned to her home parish, then, and entered the
church which had been the scene of her main triumphs, she discovered that most of her old support had disappeared and that
John Cotton himself stood at the head of the room ready to act
as her prosecutor.

In many ways, the church trial was sheer ritual. The Antinomian crisis had been settled for several months, its principal
actors either stripped of their power, banished from the colony,

[17] John Cotton, "The Way of Congregational Churches Cleared," London, 1648, in *Antinomianism in the Colony of Massachusetts Bay*, edited
by Charles Francis Adams, p. 219.

[18] Winthrop, Journal, I, p. 259.

or drawn back into the orthodox fold; yet the people of the community had apparently not yet found a clear enough name for the deviancy which had flared up among them and died. Readers of the story sometimes assume that the elders of the community must have been extremely bitter to demand so much of the already broken defendant, and it is certainly true that not even the gloomiest among them had any reason to suspect that the Hutchinson party still represented a danger to the state. But when the whole affair is seen as a ceremony and not as a test of guilt, as a demonstration rather than as an inquiry, its accents and rhythms are easier to understand.

As in the civil trial, Anne Hutchinson stood before her judges and argued with them over specific tenets of her own philosophy. It was a curious and frightening contest: the elders of the church were armed with an enormous bludgeon and were fully ready to use it, yet the only weapons Mrs. Hutchinson had thought fit to provide in her own defense were cutting edges of such precision that they were useful for little else than splitting hairs.[19]

MR. COTTON: Your first opinion laid to your charge is that the souls of all men by nature are mortal and die like beasts, and for that you allege Eccl. 3.18–21.

MRS. HUTCHINSON: I desire that place might be answered: the spirit that God gives returns.

MR. COTTON: That place speaketh that the spirit ascends upwards, so Eccles. 12.7. Man's spirit doth not return to dust as man's body doth but to God. The soul of man is immortal.

MRS. HUTCHINSON: Every man consists of soul and body. Now Adam dies not except his soul and body die, and in Heb. 4., the word is lively in operation, and divides between soul and spirit: so then the spirit that God gives man, returns to God indeed, but the soul dies. And that is the spirit Eccl. speaks of, and not of the soul. Luk. 19.10.

[19] "A Report on the Trial of Mrs. Anne Hutchinson before the Church in Boston, March, 1638," *Proceedings of the Massachusetts Historical Society*, Series II, Vol. IV, 1888, pp. 161–191.

MR. COTTON: If you would hold that Adam's soul and body dies and was not redeemed or restored by Christ Jesus it will overthrow our redemption. Both soul and body is bought with a price, Luk. 19.10. I come to seek and save what was lost, I Cor. 6th chapter, end.

MRS. HUTCHINSON: I acknowledge I am redeemed from my vain conversation and other redemptions, but it is nowhere said that he came to redeem the seed of Adam but the seed of Abraham.

MR. WILSON: I desire before you lay down your scruples that you would seriously consider of the places alleged and of that in 1 Cor. 6, end: the spirit of God needs no redemption, but he speaks there neither of God's spirit but of our spirits.

MRS. HUTCHINSON: I speak not of God's spirit now. But I will propound my main scruple and that is how a thing that is immortally miserable can be immortally happy . . . .

When we wander across the pages of this transcript we are apt to get tangled in an underbrush of words, but if we read ahead without regard for the meaning of those words we soon begin to sense a rhythmic counterpoint in the sounds of the conversation—the smooth, seasoned tones of John Cotton, the crisp logic of Anne Hutchinson, the contributions of the clerical chorus in the background, and the whole punctuated by an occasional rattle of anger from John Wilson ("I look at this opinion to be dangerous and damnable and to be no less than Sadducism and atheism and therefore to be detested"). The examination, which continued through two sittings, never lost this metric quality. The various participants seemed to be moving in cadence, joined together in a kind of ceremonial chant; and while this effect may be more striking to modern readers who do not understand the arguments being exchanged, it is easy to imagine that the Boston congregation had a sense of sharing in a ritual inquisition.

Again, as is true of most such rituals, the outcome was never in serious doubt; the problem was to find a meaningful way to register it. The clergy were trying to persuade Mrs. Hutchinson to revoke her opinions, since that was the traditional role assigned them in the ceremony, and this they did according to the canons of their profession. But at the second session of the trial, an unexpected thing happened. Mrs. Hutchinson had been listening to the words of the ministers with special care and had been the center of much attention in the week between the two trial sessions, and all at once she began to wonder whether the ministers were not correct after all! This was a crucial moment, for the official formula of the ceremony called for a gentle priesthood to show their wayward sister the error of her ways and help her to repent; but what would happen at this late stage if such an event actually took place? It was simply too late for contrition, and the elders had little choice but to reverse their strategy and declare that her sudden "confession" was not very convincing. And so a new chorus of voices took over the hearing, one pointing out that no real "humiliation" was evident in her manner, another observing that "repentance is not in her face," and a third adding "for though she hath made some show of repentance yet it doth not seem to be cordial and sincere." In the end, the clergy were so reluctant to accept her change of heart that they accused her of lying about it, and this, finally, was the charge for which she was excommunicated. It was John Wilson who read the awful sentence:

For inasmuch as you, Mrs. Hutchinson, have highly transgressed and offended, and forasmuch as you have so many ways troubled the church with your errors and have drawn away many a poor soul, and have upheld your revelations: and forasmuch as you have made a lie, etc. Therefore in the name of our Lord Jesus Christ and in the name of the church I do not only pronounce you worthy to be cast out, but I do cast you out, and in the name of Christ I do deliver you up to Satan, that you may learn no more to blaspheme, to seduce, and to lie; and I do account you from this time forth to be a heathen and a publican and so to be held of all the brethren and sisters of this congregation and of others. Therefore I command you in the name of Christ Jesus and of this church as a leper to withdraw yourself out of the congregation; that as formerly you have despised and contemned the Holy Ordinances of God, and turned your back on them, so you may now have no part in them nor benefit from them.

Shortly after the church trial, Governor Winthrop wrote in his journal: "After she was excommunicated, her spirits, which seemed before to be somewhat dejected, revived again, and she gloried in her sufferings, saying, that it was the greatest happiness, next to Christ, that ever befell her. Indeed, it was a happy day to the churches of Christ here, and to many poor souls who had been seduced by her, who . . . were (through the grace of God) brought off quite from her errors, and settled in the truth." [20]

Although it is convenient to place Mrs. Hutchinson in the center of the Antinomian controversy and describe the whole affair as if it were somehow an extension of her unusual character, no amount of personal biography can explain by itself the events which led to her banishment. Our problem is not to learn why a woman of her odd opinions and leanings should appear in seventeenth-century Boston, but rather why the people of the colony should become so alarmed over the brittle philosophies she taught in her parlor. If, as Winthrop thought, she had "seduced" the good people of Boston by her crafty conceits, it was only because they were ready for that kind of diversion anyway; and thus it is far more important to understand the shifts of mood that made the settlers responsive to her arguments than to understand the manner in which she presented them. People like Mrs. Hutchinson can be found anywhere, driven to a deep excitement by the urgency of their own convictions. They become leaders of insurrections or prophets of change only when the community around them begins to listen to the words they have been repeating all along, and then they are apt to become captives of their own unexpected audience. In 1636 the townsfolk of Boston decided to join her in her lonely crusade, and in doing so placed her in the midst of a crucial historical crossroads.

This crossroads was not marked by familiar signs, for the people of the Bay were not really aware that they had reached

[20] Winthrop, Journal, I, p. 259.

it. Puritan theory in New England had begun to change: it had lost much of its original emphasis on individual religious experience in order to promote the newer doctrine of "preparation" for salvation, which Miller has called "the peculiar badge of New England's theology," [21] and as a result, the whole notion of grace no longer had the same intimacy or the same revolutionary force. This was a change which could not be explained easily. Massachusetts Bay was a community which owed its origins to the idea that church and state should be separate, a community which had pioneered the decentralization of ecclesiastical authority, a community fashioned in the belief that each person was primarily responsible to the promptings of his own conscience; and in such a community there were no theories or traditions to relate what had happened to the New England Way, no vocabulary of words to explain this shift in focus. In many ways, the magistrates' decision to banish Mrs. Hutchinson was a substitute for the words they could not find. The verdict against her was a public statement about the new boundaries of Puritanism in Massachusetts Bay, for in passing sentence on Mrs. Hutchinson the magistrates were declaring in the only way they could that the historical stage she had come to represent was now past. No simpler language was available for that purpose.

The Quaker Invasion

And so they suffered, not for a law already broken, but for one that was intended to be made.[22]

At first glance, the Quaker persecutions which began in 1656 appear to be similar to the Antinomian quarrels of twenty years

[21] Perry Miller, *The New England Mind: From Colony to Province* (Cambridge, Mass.: Harvard University Press, 1953), p. 63.

[22] George Bishop, *New England Judged by the Spirit of the Lord* (Philadelphia: Thomas Stuckey, 1885), p. 136. This work was first printed in 1703 and was written in two installments dated 1661 and 1667.

earlier. On each of these occasions the elders of Massachusetts were confronted by an elusive group of adversaries who seldom stated their case with calm reasoning but often acted as if they possessed some special insight into the mind of God. The Antinomians spoke hazily about the "covenant of grace" and the Quakers spoke in equally vague terms about an "inner light," but both were suggesting roughly the same thing: that men should engineer their own relations with God and need not submit their religious experiences to the review of any church official. In the broader sweep of American history, then, the Antinomian and Quaker episodes are often linked together, for they represent the first stirrings of a discontent which later changed the entire character of the Puritan adventure. Yet in many ways the two crime waves were altogether different. The Antinomians threatened the political outlines of the New England Way by denying that the ministers of the Bay were competent to deal with the mysterious workings of grace, while the Quakers challenged the very notion of an orthodox community by pressing for religious toleration as a basic civil right. Although the men and women who took active roles in the two crises were quite alike (indeed the Quaker ranks included several people who had once been aligned with the Antinomian faction), there was an important difference in the quality and certainly in the outcome of the two events. In one sense, at least, the Antinomian controversy can be viewed as an attempt on the part of the larger community to repudiate an older and no longer meaningful brand of Puritanism, while the Quaker persecutions can be viewed as an attempt to resist the appearance of a newer one.

Looking back over three centuries, it seems that Massachusetts responded to the Quaker menace with a harshness quite out of proportion to the danger it actually posed. The first Quakers to arrive in the colony were a pair of middle-aged housewives who sailed quietly into Boston Bay, yet the authorities met this modest challenge with such an imposing show of strength that they were later chided for acting "as if a formidable army had invaded your borders." [23] In more than one respect this response was not so unreasonable as it may appear, for the two women had floated into Boston on the crest of a worldwide reaction against the very kind of orthodoxy the settlers were trying to establish, and the magistrates greeted these first missionaries with exactly the same hospitality they would have shown an armed battalion of demons.

Our information about the Quaker persecutions in New England is sketchy at best. The most thorough document on the subject is a book written in 1661 and enlarged in 1667 by George Bishop, an English Quaker who gathered a good deal of material from associates who had journeyed to Massachusetts. Bishop's book was written as a protest against the government of the Bay and is in no sense an objective review of the issue; yet there are a number of instances throughout the text where Bishop's information can be checked against other documents, and in each of these cases his narrative proves to be essentially accurate. The tone of the book is partisan and exceedingly angry, but the facts it reports are generally accepted by historians as valid. A second body of data on the Quaker persecutions comes from the records of the Massachusetts colony itself. In the present section these records will be cited more frequently than is the case elsewhere in the study, for they supply our only view of the way in which the authorities felt about the odd "invasion" which broke on their shores.

I

When the Quakers first appeared in Massachusetts the colony was facing a number of serious changes. To begin with, the first generation of leaders had largely disappeared from the scene, leaving the government in newer and rougher hands. Winthrop had died in 1649, Cotton in 1652, and many of their

---

[23] *Ibid.*

original colleagues had either followed them to the grave or had gone back to England with the outbreak of the Civil War. Moreover, the flow of immigrants into the Bay area had virtually stopped with the emergence of a more favorable political climate in England, and as a result Massachusetts had lost many of its most important contacts with the rest of the world.

In many respects, John Winthrop's death marked the end of an age. The community he had worked so hard to establish was now organized along very formal lines: an explicit code of law had been published in 1648 to provide the colony with a legal frame, the Cambridge Platform had been adopted in the same year to give the churches an explicit constitution, and in general the sense of inspiration which had once given the community its main force and vigor was now converted into a group of neatly shaped institutions. The dimensions of the New England Way had been reproduced in blueprint form, channeling the life of the community along highly structured avenues. The burning issues of the first generation were resolved (or so the colonists seemed to think) and the second generation was learning how to live within this framework. "New England was no longer a reformation," Perry Miller writes, "it was an administration." [24]

Perhaps the most significant change that had taken place, however, was the gradual isolation of Massachusetts Bay from its sources of support in England, a development which can only be understood by taking a brief look at what was happening in the old country.

When the Puritan forces in England finally took the field against their King they found themselves divided into two general groups—the Presbyterian moderates who wanted to form a national church along Scottish lines and the Congregational Independents who sought a loose federation of local churches somewhat after the model of New England. The Presbyterians were

[24] Perry Miller, *The New England Mind: From Colony to Province* (Cambridge, Mass.: Harvard University Press, 1953), p. 11.

strong in Parliament itself and drew a measure of support from the rising commercial classes, while the Independents were deeply concentrated in the ranks of Cromwell's army and enjoyed a considerable popularity throughout the country as a whole. Thus the English political situation became quite confused as soon as the Rebellion got underway, and on the very eve of victory the war turned into a triangular contest between Parliament, the army, and the once defeated King.

When Cromwell finally emerged into power, Massachusetts rejoiced: this was the moment for which the saints had been waiting, the reformation they had worked so hard to achieve, and for a time it seemed that their grandest dreams had been realized. Independents in England began to describe their program as the "New England Way" and even invited a group of Massachusetts clergymen to journey to London for consultation and advice. It seemed that the people of the Bay were about to play the historic role for which God's commission had prepared them.

No sooner had Massachusetts Bay sent messages of congratulation back to England, however, when the colony had to recoil in shock, for it soon became apparent that the Puritans of Cromwell's army were a wholly different breed of men than their brothers in the Bay. They had talked a rough brand of philosophy during the long campaign and had returned from the wars with an almost comradely willingness to tolerate any kind of religious opinion; and to make matters worse, they were listening with respect to people like Roger Williams and Henry Vane who had learned all the wrong lessons from the New England experience. Thus the settlers of the Bay could only turn away in disgust as the idea of toleration took slow root in the soil they had tried to claim as their own. Nathaniel Ward stated the Massachusetts position on this matter with characteristic emphasis:

First, such as have given or taken any unfriendly reports of us New English should do well to recollect themselves. We have been reputed to be a colluvies of wild opinionists, swarmed into a remote wilderness to find elbow room for our fanatic doctrines and practices. I trust our diligence past and constant sedulity against such persons and courses will plead better things for us. I dare to take upon me to be the herald of New England as far as to proclaim to the world, in the name of our colony, that all Familists, Antinomians, Anabaptists, and other enthusiasts shall have free liberty to keep away from us; and such as will come, to be gone as fast as they can, the sooner the better.[25]

"The conscious point" of this work by Ward, Perry Miller tells us, "is that American experience had come to mean, or rather remained, something different from England's." [26] And as a result, the colony found itself cut off from the stream of history it had planned to supervise, and was left far behind as a lonely pocket of reaction while England swept ahead into the modern world. This reversal was caught very sharply in the title of a contemporary pamphlet: "Ill Newes from New-England, Wherein is declared that while old England is becoming new, New-England is become old." [27]

The trouble was that the colony had lost its main reason for existing. The saints had come to the new world to provide an object lesson for the rest of mankind, and when the English Puritans lost interest in the model which Massachusetts had offered for their instruction, the whole project seemed a little pointless. Again, Perry Miller puts it well:

If an actor, playing the leading role in the greatest dramatic spectacle of the century, were to attire himself and put on his make-up, rehearse his lines, take a deep breath, and stride onto the stage, only to find the theater dark and empty, no spotlight working, and him-

[25] Nathaniel Ward, "The Simple Cobler of Aggawam," London, 1647, found in *The American Puritans,* edited by Perry Miller (New York: Doubleday Anchor, 1956), pp. 96–97.

[26] Miller, *The New England Mind: From Colony to Province,* p. 123.

[27] John Clark, "Ill Newes from New-England . . ." London, 1652, *Collections of the Massachusetts Historical Society,* Fourth Series, II, 1854.

self entirely alone, he would feel as did New England around 1650 or 1660. For in the 1640's during the Civil War, the colonies, so to speak, lost their audience.[28]

And thus the people of Massachusetts had to face a serious problem of identity. "Who, they are forever asking themselves, who are we?—and sometimes they are on the verge of saying, who the Devil are we, anyway?" [29] The settlers had stepped outside the historical momentum which was slowly drawing the rest of the English-speaking world into a general era of toleration, and for that reason they were no longer able to look to the Puritan movement in England for help in assessing their place in the universe. The appearance of the Quakers in America, then, had a special meaning for the settlers: whatever else New England might be in these uncertain times, it was most assuredly not a place which encouraged freedom of religion, and this was a distinguishing trait which the settlers meant to publicize, literally, for all they were worth. For the moment, at least, this was almost the only identity they could claim.

Moreover, the colony had new leaders well equipped for that kind of work. The constructive atmosphere which had once been generated by Winthrop and Cotton had been replaced by the far less restrained influence of men like John Endicott and John Norton, who succeeded as chief magistrate and chief clergyman, respectively. These men inherited the programs and policies of the Winthrop era, but they adopted a posture of defense rather than one of growth, protecting the legacy which had been left them rather than shaping it to suit the needs of the changing times. The honest doubts which once turned Winthrop to his journal with questions about policy and procedure were now replaced by a mood of absolute certainty. Endicott, says Brooks Adams in a passage which could serve to describe John Norton

[28] Perry Miller, *Errand in the Wilderness* (Cambridge, Mass.: Harvard University Press, 1960), p. 13.
[29] *Ibid.*, p. 15.

as well, "was almost heroic in his ferocious bigotry and daring, a perfect champion of the church." [30]

Thus Massachusetts completed the cycle which had begun when Winthrop lost his argument against the legal code. During his long tenure as the leader of Massachusetts, Winthrop had seen the subjective principles of Puritanism slowly hardened into a solid network of institutions, and now, only a few years after his death, these same principles had become the frozen heritage of a new and far less versatile generation. If Winthrop can be called the architect of the Puritan commonwealth, then Endicott was its caretaker, guarding the structure against intruders and taking stubborn care that its traditional furniture remained securely in place. Historically, this kind of behavior is often associated with people who are no longer sure of their own place in the world, people who need to protect their old customs and ways all the more narrowly because they seem to have a difficult time remembering quite who they are.

II

We do not know very much about the people who took part in the Quaker persecutions of 1656–1665. Several dozen Quakers came to the Bay during that time, traveling overground from Rhode Island or arriving by ship from other ports, and these were joined in their missionary efforts by a large number of local converts. We know the names of a few and we know what happened to several others during the decade of trouble, but we have only a vague idea where most of them came from or where they eventually went. And so any description of the affair is apt to take on the flavor of a military chronicle: we seem to be dealing with anonymous troops rather than individual persons, with

[30] Brooks Adams, *Emancipation of Massachusetts: The Dream and the Reality,* second edition (New York: Houghton Mifflin, 1919), p. 273.

campaigns rather than civil demonstrations—all of which may help us understand why the participants on both sides seemed to think they were engaged in a great religious war. The raw militancy of the Quakers certainly contributed to the notion that they were a disciplined army in the service of Satan, and for their own part, the Puritan saints quite naturally assumed that any adversary who challenged their way of life must be part of an organized attack on Christianity. Yet this picture is not satisfactory from a sociological point of view. There is little evidence of organization anywhere in those unruly ranks, aside from the efforts of a few experienced missionaries, and on the whole it is safer to assume that most of the men and women who later became known as Quakers neither knew one another very well nor planned their activities with a very keen eye for tactics. Again, a crime wave was set into motion because the community became concerned about the behavior of some of its members, and once that feeling of alarm had been expressed, people swarmed to the battle line which had been drawn.

Although the General Court had once ordered that any Quaker literature found in the colony should be publicly burned, the first open indication of trouble did not occur until 1656 when the two Quaker housewives were found in Boston Bay. The authorities had apparently been warned of their arrival, for the women were arrested even before they had time to disembark from the ship. They were promptly taken to jail, where they were stripped of their clothing and searched for marks of witchcraft; and the next day the books they had brought with them were publicly burned in the market place. Not long afterward they were joined in prison by a group of eight or nine other missionaries who had followed them into the Bay, and after a long detention (during which the windows of the jail were boarded to prevent contact with passers-by) the entire group was thrown aboard outgoing ships and hurried back to Barbados. Seen as a military operation, this first encounter with the Quakers was smoothly handled, and we may presume that the authorities were pleased enough with the outcome; but there was one technicality that did cause a word of comment among some of the more thoughtful citizens, and this had to do with the fact that there were as yet no laws in the Bay prohibiting Quaker activities.

This problem was immediately corrected. In October, 1656, a law against "that cursed sect of heretics lately risen up in the world" was enacted by the colony's General Court and published "in several places of Boston, by beat of drum." This order provided stiff fines for any ship owners or captains who knowingly brought Quakers into the jurisdiction and even stiffer penalties for settlers who sheltered Quaker missionaries or repeated Quaker "blasphemies." The order went on to state: "Lastly, it is hereby ordered, that what person or persons soever shall revile the office or persons of magistrates or ministers, as is usual with the Quakers, such persons shall be severely whipped or pay the sum of five pounds." [31] It should perhaps be pointed out in passing that most Quakers would refuse to pay such a fine as a matter of conscience, so that the punishment for being a Quaker (or more correctly for acting like one!) was in fact a flogging. Also, one of the most curious features of this resolution is that it says nothing whatever about banishment. Apparently the government of Massachusetts had not yet become concerned about local defectors to the Quaker cause, for the resolution was primarily addressed to foreign visitors who could be sent away without formal banishment proceedings.

If the law of 1656 had any effect on the Quakers, it was only to spur them into more vigorous activity. Before long a full-scale program of infiltration had been launched against the colony, led by men and women who asked for nothing more than a chance for martyrdom, and the effort soon began to pay off by producing local converts. Perhaps the most embarrassing thing about this newer wave of Quaker activity was that several of the people involved had already tasted Puritan justice and evi-

[31] Massachusetts Records, IVa, pp. 277–278.

dently had developed a roaring appetite for more. To the authorities themselves, this could only mean that the present laws were not sufficiently harsh; in 1657, accordingly, the General Court put sharper teeth in its provisions against the Quakers and this time took notice of the obvious fact that many of the culprits were residents of the colony.

And it is further ordered, that if any Quaker or Quakers shall presume, after they have once suffered what the law requireth, to come into this jurisdiction, every such male Quaker shall for the first offense have one of his ears cut off, and be kept at work in the house of correction till he can be sent away at his own charge, and for the second offense shall have his other ear cut off, and kept in the house of correction, as aforesaid; and every woman Quaker that hath suffered the law here and shall presume to come into this jurisdiction shall be severely whipped, and kept at the house of correction at work till she be sent away at her own charge, and so for her coming again she shall be alike used as aforesaid; and for every Quaker, he or she, that shall a third time herein again offend, they shall have their tongues bored through with a hot iron, and kept at the house of correction, close to work, till they be sent away at their own charge. And it is further ordered, that all and every Quaker arising from amongst ourselves shall be dealt with and suffer the like punishment as the law provides against foreign Quakers.[32]

Three persons lost an ear for infringing this law, but the pace of the attack continued to increase at a fearful rate and with it the volume of punishment which the authorities were ready to dispense. There were many beatings, imprisonments, fines, and various other forms of harassment. One William Brend, who had been with the first group of Quakers to appear in Massachusetts, was reputedly beaten with 117 blows from a corded whip, a flogging so serious that the local physician simply left him for dead. As Bishop describes the event, ". . . his flesh was beaten black and as into jelly, and under his arms the bruised flesh and blood hung down, clotted as it were into bags; and it was so beaten into one mass, that the signs of one particular blow

[32] Massachusetts Records, IVa, pp. 308–309.

could not be seen." [33] This account may exaggerate Brend's injuries, but it does not for a moment exaggerate the mood of vicious anger which prevailed throughout the colony.

These grisly episodes only increased the excitement of the people of the Bay, drawing some of them into a more forceful attitude of persecution and others into a deeper sympathy with the Quaker movement. By this time there were perhaps two dozen foreigners traveling around the countryside in an effort to stir up dissention and a hundred or more local converts who met together for religious meetings. In early 1658, for example, the constables raided a house in Salem and arrested nineteen inhabitants of the town who had met there with two foreign missionaries. [34] Subsequent records of the county court indicate that this cell continued to meet in one fashion or another for many years and soon grew to a membership of over fifty people —quite a considerable number in so small a town.

When the General Court assembled for its annual meeting in October of 1658, then, the authorities were in a desperate mood. Every measure they had taken to discourage the Quakers only seemed to provoke them into more vigorous action, and with the single-mindedness that often characterized Puritan thinking they decided to make the penalties against Quakers even more severe than was already the case. The new law provided that anyone guilty of Quaker disorders would be banished from the territory "upon pain of death." [35] The wording of the law, then, implied that Quaker crimes were only to be punished by banishment, but that failure to honor the conditions of banishment would itself be regarded a capital offense. Whether the court appreciated it or not, this order was almost an open invita-

[33] Bishop, *New England Judged*, p. 57.

[34] *Records and Files of the Quarterly Courts of Essex County, Massachusetts, 1636–1682,* edited by George Francis Dow (Salem, Mass.: The Essex Institute), II, pp. 103–104. (Cited throughout the study as Essex County Records.)

[35] Massachusetts Records, IVa, pp. 345–346.

tion to disaster, for nothing could so satisfy the Quakers' call to persecution as a chance to suffer on the gallows for the sake of conscience.

As a result, candidates for execution rushed toward the arena from every corner of New England, among them people who had felt the constable's whip, who had spent long months in the Boston jail, who had suffered the loss of all their property, and at least two who had lost an ear on the block. The authorities responded to the new attack by stepping up the pace of their own persecutions. In May of 1659 the General Court banished six inhabitants of Salem under the provisions of the new law,[36] and shortly thereafter sold two young children into bondage to satisfy claims against their parents.[37] But each act of hostility on the part of the magistrates only seemed to charge their opposition with new energy, and by the summer of 1659 it was apparent that Massachusetts would either have to retreat to a more moderate position or seal its determination with a real display of blood. The least that can be said for both parties is that they were equal to the challenge.

Several Quakers who had been banished on pain of death returned to Boston during a meeting of the General Court in a deliberate test of the new law. With them came a whole retinue of followers, including a group of settlers from Salem (one of whom had joined the procession "to bring linen wherein to wrap the dead bodies of those who were to suffer"),[38] several Quakers from Rhode Island who came to visit a colleague in prison, and a number of other people who for one reason or another were not under lock and key themselves. The whole company, well over twenty persons, was immediately thrown into the Boston jail to join an unknown number of Quakers already there. "All these," Bishop explained to the Massachusetts officials, "as one, came together, in the moving and power of the Lord, to look

[36] Massachusetts Records, IVa, p. 367.
[37] Bishop, *New England Judged*, p. 89.
[38] *Ibid.*, p. 99.

your bloody laws in the face, and to accompany those who should suffer by them." [39]

The Court responded to this summons by selecting three persons from the crowd in prison and sentencing them to death—William Robinson, Marmaduke Stevenson, and a woman named Mary Dyer who was remembered in Massachusetts as one of Anne Hutchinson's most loyal adherents. Bishop relates that the completely frustrated Endicott, "speaking faintly, as a man whose life was departing from him," seemed overwhelmed at the trial. "We have made many laws, and endeavored by several ways to keep you from us," he is supposed to have said, "and neither whipping nor imprisonment, nor cutting off ears, nor banishment upon pain of death, will keep you from among us. . . . I desire not your deaths." [40] Whether or not the Governor actually spoke those plaintive lines, the records of the Court only mention that he pronounced sentence on the three defendants: "you shall go from hence to the place from whence you came, and from thence to the place of execution, and there hang till you be dead." It is interesting to notice that the Court also ordered one hundred militia men, "completely armed with pike, and musket, with powder and bullet, to lead them to the place of execution, and there see them hang till they be dead." [41] Evidently the authorities were not at all confident that their hard judgment would be popular among the aroused people of Boston.

At the execution, Bishop tells us, a familiar face appeared in the crowd. John Wilson was now a haunted old man who had recently told his congregation that he would "carry fire in one hand, and faggots in the other, to burn all the Quakers in the world." As the procession moved toward the gallows, led by a hundred armed soldiers and a squad of drummers, Wilson sprang from the gathering and accosted William Robinson. "Shall such jacks as you come in before authority with your hats on?" he

[39] *Ibid.*, p. 99.
[40] *Ibid.*, pp. 99–100.
[41] Massachusetts Records, IVa, p. 383.

jeered. "Mind you," Robinson is supposed to have said, "mind you, it is for the not putting off the hat that we are put to death." And later, when Robinson and Stevenson were trying to say a last few words to the Boston audience and the drummers were hammering away in an effort to drown them out, Wilson's voice could be heard over the rest of the din: "Hold thy tongue, be silent! Thou art going to die with a lie in thy mouth." [42] When the noise and confusion had reached a crescendo, Mary Dyer was suddenly taken down from the scaffold and reprieved. We know that government officials from Rhode Island had been trying to save her life, and perhaps this was an important factor in the magistrates' decision; but we also know that the Boston crowd was growing restless at the sight of the three condemned Quakers lined up on the scaffold and may have been ready to interfere.

Whatever prompted the authorities to spare Mary Dyer, it is not difficult to imagine that they might have felt a little uneasy. Almost the whole town had come to witness the spectacle and the market place was alive with crackling new sights and sounds —soldiers marching in cadence with loaded muskets, drummers tapping out a sharp staccato beat, mourners carrying winding sheets and issuing frightful warnings to the crowd, incendiaries like Wilson circulating among the onlookers and urging the hangman to do his best, and in the midst of all this, the prisoners themselves, walking along hand in hand with the exultant look of persons who have waited a long time for martyrdom. The effect of this scene would not likely be lost on any of its witnesses.

The two executions, of course, did little to discourage Quaker activities in the Bay, but the excitement generated on that one day in Boston reverberated throughout the territory for a long time. On the one hand, it inspired local constables to prodigious feats of persecution, and in the months that followed, the number of confiscations, household raids, public floggings, and the

[42] Bishop, *New England Judged*, pp. 102–103.

like were greatly increased. On the other hand, however, the Quakers began to parade their eccentricities before the magistrates with an abandon that must have seemed incredible to those austere men. It is easy to condemn the authorities of Massachusetts for their pointless cruelty and narrow vision during the Quaker crisis, but the difficulty they faced was an extremely awkward one, as these citations from the records of one county court testify:

John Burton, coming into court in an uncivil manner, reproached the court by saying they were robbers and destroyers of the widows and fatherless, that their priests divined for money and their worship was not the worship of God, interrupting and affronting the court, and upon being commanded to silence, commanded them to silence and continued speaking until the court was fain to commit him to the stocks.[43]

The wife of Robert Wilson, for her barbarous and inhuman going naked through the town, is sentenced to be tied at a cart's tail with her body naked downward to her waist, and whipped from Mr. Gidney's gate till she come to her own house, not exceeding thirty stripes . . . .[44]

Lydia Wardell was ordered to be severely whipped and to pay costs to the Marshall of Hampton upon her presentment for going naked into Newbury meeting house.[45]

And Thomas Hutchinson, writing more than a hundred years afterward, knew of other examples:

At Boston one George Wilson, and at Cambridge one Elizabeth Horton, went crying through the streets that the Lord was coming with fire and sword to plead with them. Thomas Newhouse went into the meeting house at Boston with a couple of glass bottles and broke them before the congregation, and threatened, "Thus will the Lord break you in pieces." Another time M. Brewster came in with her face smeared and black as coal . . . . One Faubord, of Grindleton, carried his enthusiasm still higher and was sacrificing his son in imi-

[43] Essex County Records, II, p. 337.
[44] Essex County Records, III, p. 17.
[45] Essex County Records, III, p. 64.

tation of Abraham, but the neighbors hearing the lad cry, broke open the house and happily prevented it.[46]

Shortly after the executions of Robinson and Stevenson, the General Court published a short declaration about its proceedings which was probably meant for circulation in England. Explaining that the Court was only attempting to defend itself against the "impudent and insolent obtrusions" of the Quakers, the declaration concluded:

The consideration of our gradual proceedings will vindicate us from the clamorous accusations of severity, our own just and necessary defense calling upon us, other means failing, to offer the point, which these persons have violently and willfully rushed upon, and thereby become *felons de se* [in effect, guilty of suicide] . . . .[47]

And indeed it did sometimes seem that the Quakers were running headlong onto the spear which the magistrates had planted in front of them. In the two years following the deaths of Robinson and Stevenson large numbers of people earned eligibility for the gallows by returning to the colony after once being sentenced to banishment, and although the Court was aware that the hangings had not been very popular in the colony as a whole, it was deeply committed to that line of action. In 1660, after many months of effort, Mary Dyer finally reached the goal she had sought so long and was hung in Boston. In 1661 she was followed to the grave by an energetic missionary named William Leddra. These two victims, however, represented but a fraction of the Quakers who had made themselves available for execution, and when the waiting list for trial had grown to an impossible length it was evident that the Bay colony would either have to develop new tactics or initiate one of the bloodiest massacres on record.

At the time of Leddra's execution there were some twenty-seven persons in the Boston jail and enough Quakers scattered

[46] Hutchinson, *History*, I, pp. 203–204.
[47] "A Declaration of the General Court of the Massachusetts," October, 1659, reprinted in Mather, *Magnalia*, pp. 525–526.

throughout the countryside to fill several other prisons of equal size. In the hopes of clearing out this overflow, the Court passed a new resolution against the Quakers which soon became known as the "vagabond act." The law provided that all itinerant wayfarers who wandered around the colony "like rogues and vagabonds" were to be

stripped naked from the middle upwards, and tied to a cart's tail and whipped through the town, and from thence immediately conveyed to the constable of the next town toward the borders of our jurisdiction . . . and so from constable to constable till they be conveyed through any the outward-most towns of our jurisdiction.[48]

The campaign against the Quakers seems to have lost much of its momentum when the vagabond act went into effect. Although Bishop reports that some ferocious beatings took place as the constables carried out their new orders, much of the crusading spirit went out of the battle on both sides of the firing line. Moreover, the authorities were soon to learn that their urgent drive against the Quakers would have to slacken off in any case. In late 1661 the Court received a letter from Charles II prohibiting the use of either corporal or capital punishment in cases involving the Quakers, and this announcement stopped the magistrates quite in their tracks. The Court wrote a few lame protests into the record and bewailed the fact that their monarch was so poorly informed about the matter, but in the end they had no choice but to suspend all laws currently in force against the Quakers.[49]

The persecution of Quakers in Massachusetts Bay did not really end with the arrival of the King's letter, particularly since the vagabond law could be used without applying the label "Quaker" at all, but from that moment the intensity of the struggle steadily diminished. As soon as the Quakers saw that their adversaries were no longer armed with a license to execute, they

[48] Massachusetts Records, IVb, pp. 2–3.
[49] The King's letter is reproduced in Bishop, *New England Judged*, p. 214, and the reaction of the court is found in Massachusetts Records, IVb, p. 34.

gradually lost interest in the project, suggesting to what extent a forceful definition of deviance may attract potential offenders. Somehow the whole contest was less attractive to both sides once its rules had become more civilized.

As early as 1657 a prominent citizen of the Bay had noted in his diary that Quakers only seemed to enjoy the process of stirring up trouble when they ran a better than even chance of getting hurt as a consequence. "They seem to suffer patiently, and even take a kind of pleasure in it. In those parts of the country where they might with freedom converse (as in Rhode Island and Providence and Warwick) they take no pleasure to be." [50] And the government of Rhode Island, writing in 1657 to the authorities of the Bay, made essentially the same observation:

Concerning these Quakers (so called) which are now among us, we have no law among us whereby to punish any . . . . And we, moreover, find, that in those places where these people aforesaid, in this colony, are most of all suffered to declare themselves freely, and are only opposed by arguments in discourse, there they least of all desire to come, and we are informed that they begin to loathe this place, for that they are not opposed by the civil authority, but with all patience and meekness are suffered to say over their pretended revelations and admonitions, nor are they like or able to gain many here to their way; and surely we find that they delight to be persecuted by civil powers, and when they are so, they are like to gain more adherents by the conceit of their patient sufferings, than by consent to their pernicious sayings. [51]

Comparing the policies adopted by the authorities of Massachusetts with those found in Rhode Island, we can see an important relationship between deviant behavior and the boundaries of the community. The Quaker movement was nourished by the cruelties of its enemies and could not easily survive once that opposition had been withdrawn. Now this was a lesson the more tolerant colonies to the south, tempered by men like William Coddington or Roger Williams, could afford to learn; but it was

[50] John Hull's Diary, *Transactions and Collections of the American Antiquarian Society* (Boston: Printed by the Society, 1857), p. 182.

[51] Hutchinson, *History*, I, Appendix XI, pp. 526–527.

not a lesson which the authorities of the Bay were in any position to understand. To accept the Quakers, even if that proved the most effective way of curbing their disorderly activities, would mean to repudiate one of the fundamental ideas on which the New England Way was then based. The Quaker crusade was an exhibit of great importance to the people of the Bay, and the means they chose to combat it did far more to publicize that crusade than to curtail it.

In the end, then, both sides withdrew from the field when the war began to lose its more violent edges, leaving later historians to speculate what the contest had been all about in the first place. One historian observed that "Puritans and Quakers were so much alike that we think at once of the old saying: there are no enemies so bitter as variants of the same species," [52] and there is something to be said for this point. It was exactly because the New England Puritans shared so many features in common with the Quakers that they had to publicize the few crucial differences as noisily as they could. The settlers of the Bay were turning away from a historical and cultural ethic that the Quaker movement had come to symbolize, and in order to mark off a new set of boundaries for the New England Way they had to make a particular effort to emphasize those points where the Puritan and Quaker streams diverged. The differences between them may appear quite small when measured by the standards of another century, but for the moment, at least, they happened to be the differences which set New England apart as a special place.

III

One of the most interesting aspects of the Quaker crisis in the Bay was that no one seemed very concerned to describe what

[52] Charles E. Park, "Puritans and Quakers," *New England Quarterly,* XXVII (1954), p. 73.

the Quakers were talking about in theological terms. Neither George Bishop's long narrative nor the surviving records of the colony devote any space to the task of explaining how the Puritans differed from their unwelcome guests, and in this respect the Quaker dispute is quite unlike the Antinomian controversy that had flared up twenty years earlier. Literature from the period fairly crackles with angry denunciations of the Quakers, but for all the heat generated by this verbal attack it seems that the authorities neither knew very much nor cared what theories lay behind the Quaker crusade. Indeed, the people of Massachusetts were so poorly informed about Quaker beliefs that they could not even identify their opponents on that basis. The major distinguishing traits used by the Puritans to pick Quakers out of the crowd (and this was as true in courts of law as in ordinary conversations) had nothing whatever to do with creeds or doctrines: Quakers were persons who wore hats in the presence of magistrates, used terms like "thee" and "thou" when speaking to single individuals, and sometimes gathered together for private religious services. In principle, to be sure, the authorities only used these identifying symbols as means for recognizing Quakers and not as grounds for punishing them, but many people in the Bay were quick to point out that the Quakers were not really accused of much else during the entire decade of crisis. A few examples may be instructive, for if nothing else, they indicate very clearly how small tokens and insignia can come to mean a great deal when a community begins to label its deviant members.

In 1656, when the first two Quakers landed in Boston, they were quickly brought before Deputy Governor Bellingham for questioning, and he seems to have committed them to jail the first time one of them used the word "thee" in the conversation: "I need no more," he is supposed to have said to the constable, "now I see they are Quakers." [53] A short time later a group of

[53] Bishop, *New England Judged*, p. 11.

Quakers was brought into court on a charge of blasphemy and began to argue that the accusation was wholly without basis. Apparently the magistrates were having a difficult time finding a legitimate foundation for the charge, and when the conversation had wandered off into a wilderness of technicalities, Simon Bradstreet brought it back with a masterful piece of New England reasoning: "the court will find out an easier way to find out a Quaker than by blasphemy—the not putting off the hat." [54] And finally, this exchange is supposed to have taken place between an unidentified magistrate and a local convert to Quakerism named Edward Wharton:

WHARTON: Friends, what is the cause and wherefore have I been fetched from my habitation, where I was following my honest calling, and here laid up as an evil-doer?

MAGISTRATE: Your hair is too long and you are disobedient to that commandment which saith, "Honor thy mother and father."

WHARTON: Wherein?

MAGISTRATE: In that you will not put off your hat before the magistrates. [55]

These anecdotes were all reported by Bishop, which may give us sufficient reason to doubt their accuracy, but judging what we otherwise know about the Puritan authorities none of them seem unlikely. It might be remembered that the first resolution enacted against Quakers was concerned with people "who revile the office or persons of magistrates or ministers, as is usual with the Quakers"—perhaps an admission that the Court knew no other method to identify this odd brand of heretic. Moreover, the surviving records of the colony do not supply one case in which a defendant's convictions were ever discussed in court. The first wave of Quakers to appear before the bench were convicted of crimes like contempt of authority, failure to attend the church services, and other kinds of misdemeanor; but once the

[54] *Ibid.*, p. 71.
[55] *Ibid.*, pp. 198–199.

cycle of persecution had been set in motion it provided its own momentum. A number of floggings took place as a result of failure to pay fines, and of course the four executions occurred because the victims defied court orders to keep out of the country. Technically speaking, these crimes had nothing to do with religious activities at all.

In this sense, the Puritan authorities would seem to have been far more concerned about the outer forms of the Quaker unrest than they were with its inner motives, and this, too, is an apt reflection of the age. During the Antinomian controversy the community leaders spent a good deal of time trying to understand the peculiar humors which compelled people like Anne Hutchinson and her more active followers to behave so strangely. They did not approach this task with any kindness or sympathy, of course, but they displayed an honest interest in learning something about the emotional tone of the protest and the inner condition of the men and women who participated in it. Twenty years later, however, when the Quakers swept onto the scene, this type of concern had largely disappeared. Throughout the late 1650's the magistrates of Massachusetts expressed only the faintest concern with the spirit of the Quaker crusade or the convictions of its adherents, so little that they rarely inquired about the motives which drove the Quakers along their reckless path. Had they done so, the whole affair might have had a different ending, for it is difficult to imagine that even the stern theocrats of the Bay could have executed people with so feeble a program as theirs.

Massachusetts' real case against the Quakers was that they did not show any outward respect for the spirit of Puritan discipline or contribute to the ritual observances of community life, and in doing so they asked for a kind of subjective freedom which the colony was in no position to confer. They were willing to live within the formal structure of the commonwealth but could not share its assumptions about spirituality; they were ready to commit their energies but not their whole hearts to the enterprise. And thus they seemed to live within the Puritan world without really becoming a part of it. They did not attend religious services regularly, and when they did they were apt to disturb the congregation by offering unsolicited remarks of their own from the audience; they did not follow the New England custom of showing special deference to the magistrates and they defied certain conventions of speech by using odd personal pronouns in their conversations with others. None of these offenses seem serious enough to warrant the hard measures taken against them, but they represented a special kind of threat to the Puritan community because they seemed to suggest a conscious lack of respect for the New England concept of authority. In the very act of living apart from the rest of the community, the Quakers had ignored a fundamental responsibility by failing to share in what Durkheim called the "collective conscience" of the group—that sense of firm ideological commitment, that willingness to participate fully in the rhythms of group life, that feeling of common heritage and common destiny which gives every society its underlying cohesion. So long as the Puritan elders suspected any Quaker of that basic betrayal, they would regard almost everything he said and did as a form of sin. An excellent example of this is again provided by Bishop:

It appears that a group of Quakers had been arrested for holding a private meeting. One of the suspects asked why he was thought to be a Quaker, and Simon Bradstreet spoke for the court, "you are one, for coming in with your hat on." Another suspect then remarked that this was a curious reason for dragging anyone into court and was told that he was really accused of blasphemy, whereupon he made the sensible suggestion that the magistrates should visit a Quaker meeting so that they "might hear, and give an account of what was done and spoken, and not conclude about a thing they knew not." At this point one Major General Dennison, a man cut from the same coarse cloth as Thomas Dudley a generation earlier, told the suspects: "If ye meet together and say anything, we may conclude ye speak blasphemy." [56] At least the General had stated the real point. It did not matter very much whether a Quaker was actually overheard muttering some spiritual indignity or other, for in the very process of remaining aloof from the ideological consensus of the community he had proved himself to be a blasphemous creature.

The saints knew little else about the Quakers, but they were quite confident (as Winthrop had said during the Antinomian controversy) "that two so opposite parties could not contain in the same body without apparent hazard of the whole." Again it was Major General Dennison who explained this point to the Quakers. During the trial of six local Quakers from Salem, Governor Endicott was asked to cite the "real and true cause" of the persecutions, and he answered briefly, "it is for contemning authority, in not coming to the ordinances of God." When one of the defendants began to protest that the maximum penalty for that offense allowed by law was a fine, Dennison interrupted to say in the plainest possible words that the court was not a whit concerned with such technicalities: "As I have told you before," he said, "you and we are not able well to live together; and, at present, the power is in our hands, and therefore the strongest must fend off." [57] The good General really had said the same thing before, and his words on that earlier occasion, too, remain in the record: "We are the stronger, and so look to yourselves." [58]

It is entertaining to think that these six defendants listened well to this lesson in power politics, for they were among the Quakers who later appealed their case to Charles II, and one of them, Samuel Shattock, was the messenger who brought the news back to Massachusetts that the crown had ordered an end to the

[56] *Ibid.*, pp. 59–60.
[57] *Ibid.*, p. 87.
[58] *Ibid.*, p. 76.

persecution. Legend tells us that Shattock delivered the King's letter personally to Endicott's house in Boston and stood there, with his hat firmly on, while the tough old Governor read it.

As was pointed out earlier, we know little about the various people who joined together in the Quaker crusade. Most of them emerged from obscurity into a fast and furious prominence, cnly to fade out of sight once the excitement of the persecutions had died away; but now and then we come across an item in the colony records which makes us wonder what happened to these people later. In 1669, for example, a brief entry is found in the minutes of the Essex County Court concerning a Mrs. Robert Wilson. Deborah Wilson was no stranger to the court, for she had appeared there many times for different Quaker offenses and had once earned a certain raw immortality by walking completely naked through the streets of Salem.

The wife of Robert Wilson, presented for frequently absenting herself from the public ordinances, was dismissed, court being informed that she is distempered in her head.[59]

And one of Mrs. Wilson's most energetic old comrades was having trouble of his own in 1674:

Whereas there is a complaint made to this court that Nathaniel Hadlock do live an idle and profuse life wandering up and down, wasting and spending his estate, whereby his wife does much suffer and like to come to misery, court declared that all persons for time to come shall neither buy nor sell nor bargain with him anything that was of his wife's estate until the court gives further order. . . .[60]

Now it is not very likely that Deborah Wilson and Nathaniel Hadlock were typical of the Quakers who troubled the peace of Massachusetts, but there is little question that the magistrates

[59] Essex County Records, IV, p. 88.
[60] Essex County Records, V, p. 356.

eventually began to think so. When the persecutions had run their course and the people of the Bay looked back on the whole episode, they came to the comfortable conclusion that the Quakers must all have been mad. With the wisdom of another half-century at his disposal, Cotton Mather offered a simple diagnosis:

I am verily persuaded these miserable Quakers would in a little while (as we have now seen) have come to nothing, if the civil had not inflicted any civil penalty upon them; nor do I look upon hereticide as an evangelical way for the extinguishing of heresies. . . . 'Tis true, these Quakers did manifest an intolerable contempt of authority, and needlessly put upon themselves a vengeance, for which the authority would have gladly released them, if they would have accepted of a release; but it is also true that they were madmen—a sort of lunatics, demoniacs and energumens . . .[61]

And over one hundred years after the execution of William Leddra in Boston, Thomas Hutchinson echoed much the same thought:

For these and such like disturbances, they might be deemed proper subjects either of a mad-house or house of correction, and it is to be lamented that any greater severities were made use of.[62]

When the people of Massachusetts reflected on the Quaker trouble, then, they defined the affair as a clash between an over-excited magistracy and a wild band of fanatics. As in the Antinomian controversy, the authorities had declared a state of emergency; men and women of every description had drifted onto the scene to participate in the skirmish that followed, and after it was all over, the boundaries of the New England Way had been visibly modified. Yet there was an important difference between the two crime waves so far as Massachusetts Bay was concerned. The Antinomian quarrel must be scored as a victory for the leading elders of the Bay because they were able to enlist

[61] Mather, *Magnalia*, p. 525.
[62] Hutchinson, *History*, I, p. 204.

support for the kind of orthodoxy they were trying to establish. But the Quaker crisis must be scored as a defeat: the Puritans deployed such a heavy concentration of men and material on the firing line in an attempt to cut off the invasion that the notion of toleration quietly moved into the vacuum left behind them and became a lasting part of the New England heritage. Only too late did they recognize that the invasion came from within, that the Quakers represented a stream of thought which was as much a part of the New England experience as the tired orthodoxy they were trying to defend. For almost a decade the colony devoted a major part of its ideological resources to the task of emphasizing Massachusetts' opposition to the idea of toleration, since this was the one distinction which separated the Puritanism of New England from the newer variant now taking root in England. And when this distinction could no longer be maintained, the settlers had little to fall back on.

For in the end, Massachusetts lost its contest with the Quakers. In the first place, local Quakers won at least a shade of the toleration they had asked for and continued to meet in private gatherings with a minimum of interference. It will be remembered, for example, that throughout the long decade of persecution a strong Quaker cell had met regularly in Salem; and in 1674, almost twenty years after the constables had staged their first raid against that stubborn group of people, they were arrested again for a "breach of law called the Quakers' meeting." This time, however, they were facing a thoroughly subdued bench of magistrates, and after an almost gentlemanly discussion of the matter were dismissed with a mild reprimand.[63] John Endicott, who was buried nearby, would have shuddered with rage.

In the second place, however, the Quakers indirectly brought about a far more telling change on the Bay colony. When Charles II returned to London in 1660 to occupy his father's throne, the

[63] Essex County Records, V, p. 298.

face of the English countryside had been unmistakably changed. The interlude of Puritan rule had nourished the sects into such vigorous activity and had spread the idea of toleration so completely that few people were willing to relinquish this freedom. In a sense, toleration had already become a tradition in England, and Charles had to realize, if vaguely, that this movement toward variety and nonconformity in the religious life of the land was irreversible. Massachusetts had seen wave after wave of banished persons travel to England to present their grievances in court, but in the generation between 1630 and 1660 no one in England was in much of a position to help them. When the Quakers brought their complaints to Charles II, however, they found a new and more sympathetic ear in Whitehall. Not only did the King bring a stop to the persecutions in Massachusetts, as we have seen, but his irritation about the matter was soon translated into something approaching a colonial policy.

In a letter dated in 1662 but not read in the General Court until 1665, the King renewed his order that "freedom and liberty of conscience" be permitted to all residents of the colony, and then delivered a massive blow to the Massachusetts orthodoxy:

We assuring ourself, and obliging and commanding all persons concerned, in the election of the Governor or Assistants, there be only consideration had of the wisdom, virtue, and integrity of the persons to be chosen, and not of any affection with reference to their opinions and outward professions, and that all freeholders of competent estate, not vicious in conversation and orthodox in religion, (though of different persuasions concerning church government,) may have their votes in the election of all officers, both civil and military. . . .[64]

With a reluctance which need only be imagined, the General Court recognized the King's authority and repealed all laws limiting the franchise to members of the church.[65]

Magistrates and ministers alike managed to interpret the

[64] Massachusetts Records, IVb, pp. 165–166.
[65] Massachusetts Records, IVb, pp. 167–168.

King's order so as to leave the formal structure of the theocracy largely intact, but with the end of the Quaker persecutions and the arrival of the royal decree from England, much of the enthusiasm that had sustained the old order seems to have silently dissipated. The commonwealth still stood, and self-appointed sentries like Increase and Cotton Mather continued to keep a more and more lonely vigil over it, but for the most part, the New England edifice was now a deserted shell. From that point to the end of the century, the settlers of the Bay gradually turned away from the original outlines of the Puritan experiment and began to look elsewhere for new sources of authority and new points of contrast. The New England Way was no longer a "city on a hill," set in conspicuous view to guide the rest of mankind toward reformation; it was no longer a bastion of defense against those evils of toleration that had torn the seams out of the Puritan movement in England. New England was only itself—and this was one role for which the settlers' theology had not prepared them.

Perhaps the shift away from theocratic discipline and toward toleration made it necessary for people to rely more on inner resources and inner safeguards, but whatever the effect of these changes, we can see a new tendency on the part of the settlers to search inside themselves for the meaningful landmarks they needed to identify the boundaries of the New England Way. On the one hand, this produced the independence and integrity, the shrewd practicality, that soon became the hallmark of the Yankee character. On the other hand, it gave the community a more individualistic focus in its search for new frames of reference—and perhaps it makes a certain kind of sense that people who begin to see discipline as a matter of *inner reliance* will also begin to see deviance as a matter of *inner possession*.

In any event, the Puritans were soon to encounter the most dreadful enemy Satan had ever sent to prey on New England: witches.

The Witches of Salem Village

The witchcraft hysteria that began in Salem Village (a town some miles away from Salem itself) is probably the best known episode of Massachusetts history and has been described in a number of careful works. In the pages which follow, then, the story will be sketched in rather briefly: readers interested in a fuller account of those unusual events are urged to consult *The Devil in Massachusetts* by Marion L. Starkey, a book that captures all the grim drama of the period without losing any of its merit as a scholarly work.[66]

Between the end of the Quaker persecutions in 1665 and the beginning of the Salem witchcraft outbreak in 1692, the colony had experienced some very trying days. To begin with, the political outlines of the commonwealth had been subject to sudden, often violent, shifts, and the people of the colony were quite uncertain about their own future. The King's decrees during the Quaker troubles had provoked only minor changes in the actual structure of the Puritan state, but they had introduced a note of apprehension and alarm which did not disappear for thirty years; and no sooner had Charles warned the Massachusetts authorities of his new interest in their affairs then he dispatched four commissioners to the Bay to look after his remote dominions and make sure that his occasional orders were being enforced. From that moment, New England feared the worst. The sermons of the period were full of dreadful prophecies about the future of the Bay, and as New England moved through the 1670's and 1680's, the catalogue of political calamities grew steadily longer and more serious. In 1670, for example, a series of harsh arguments occurred between groups of magistrates and

[66] Marion L. Starkey, *The Devil in Massachusetts* (New York: Knopf, 1949).

clergymen, threatening the alliance which had been the very cornerstone of the New England Way. In 1675 a brutal and costly war broke out with a confederacy of Indian tribes led by a wily chief called King Philip. In 1676 Charles II began to review the claims of other persons to lands within the jurisdiction of Massachusetts, and it became increasingly clear that the old charter might be revoked altogether. In 1679 Charles specifically ordered Massachusetts to permit the establishment of an Anglican church in Boston, and in 1684 the people of the Bay had become so pessimistic about the fate of the colony that several towns simply neglected to send Deputies to the General Court. The sense of impending doom reached its peak in 1686. To begin with, the charter which had given the colony its only legal protection for over half a century was vacated by a stroke of the royal pen, and in addition the King sent a Royal Governor to represent his interests in the Bay who was both an Anglican and a man actively hostile to the larger goals of New England. For the moment, it looked as if the holy experiment was over: not only had the settlers lost title to the very land they were standing on, but they ran the very real risk of witnessing the final collapse of the congregational churches they had built at so great a cost.

The settlers were eventually rescued from the catastrophes of 1686, but their margin of escape had been extremely narrow and highly tentative. In 1689 news began to filter into the Bay that William of Orange had landed in England to challenge the House of Stuart, and hopes ran high throughout the colony; but before the people of the Bay knew the outcome of this contest in England, a Boston mob suddenly rose in protest and placed the Royal Governor in chains. Luckily for Massachusetts, William's forces were successful in England and the Boston insurrection was seen as little more than a premature celebration in honor of the new King. Yet for all the furor, little had changed. At the time of the witchcraft hysteria, agents of Massachusetts were at work in London trying to convince William to restore the old charter, or at least to issue a new one giving Massachusetts all the advantages it had enjoyed in the past, but everyone knew that the colony would never again operate under the same autonomy. As the people of the Bay waited to hear about the future of their settlement, then, their anxiety was understandably high.

Throughout this period of political crisis, an even darker cloud was threatening the colony, and this had to do with the fact that a good deal of angry dissension was spreading among the saints themselves. In a colony that depended on a high degree of harmony and group feeling, the courts were picking their way through a maze of land disputes and personal feuds, a complicated tangle of litigations and suits. Moreover, the earnest attempts at unanimity that had characterized the politics of Winthrop's era were now replaced by something closely resembling open party bickering. When John Josselyn visited Boston in 1668, for instance, he observed that the people were "savagely factious" in their relations with one another and acted more out of jealousy and greed than any sense of religious purpose.[67] And the sermons of the day chose even stronger language to describe the decline in morality which seemed to darken the prospects of New England. The spirit of brotherhood which the original settlers had counted on so heavily had lately diffused into an atmosphere of commercial competition, political contention, and personal bad feeling.

Thus the political architecture which had been fashioned so carefully by the first generation and the spiritual consensus which had been defended so energetically by the second were both disappearing. At the time of the Salem witchcraft mania, most of the familiar landmarks of the New England Way had become blurred by changes in the historical climate, like signposts obscured in a storm, and the people of the Bay no longer knew

[67] John Josselyn, "An Account of Two Voyages to New-England," *Collections of the Massachusetts Historical Society,* Vol. III, Third Series, p. 331.

how to assess what the past had amounted to or what the future promised. Massachusetts had become, in Alan Heimert's words, "a society no longer able to judge itself with any certainty." [68]

In 1670, the House of Deputies took note of the confusion and fear which was beginning to spread over the country and prepared a brief inventory of the troubles facing the Bay:

Declension from the primitive foundation work, innovation in doctrine and worship, opinion and practice, an invasion of the rights, liberties and privileges of churches, an usurpation of a lordly and prelatical power over God's heritage, a subversion of the gospel order, and all this with a dangerous tendency to the utter devastation of these churches, turning the pleasant gardens of Christ into a wilderness, and the inevitable and total extirpation of the principles and pillars of the congregational way; these are the leaven, the corrupting gangrene, the infecting spreading plague, the provoking image of jealousy set up before the Lord, the accursed thing which hath provoked divine wrath, and doth further threaten destruction.[69]

The tone of this resolution gives us an excellent index to the mood of the time. For the next twenty years, New England turned more and more to the notion that the settlers must expect God to turn upon them in wrath because the colony had lost its original fervor and sense of mission. The motif introduced in this resolution runs like a recurrent theme through the thinking of the period: the settlers who had carved a commonwealth out of the wilderness and had planted "the pleasant gardens of Christ" in its place were about to return to the wilderness. But there is an important shift of imagery here, for the wilderness they had once mastered was one of thick underbrush and wild animals, dangerous seasons and marauding Indians, while the wilderness which awaited them contained an entirely different sort of peril. "The Wilderness thro' which we are passing to the

[68] Alan Heimert, "Puritanism, The Wilderness and The Frontier," *New England Quarterly*, XXVI (1953), p. 381.
[69] Hutchinson, *History*, I, p. 232. The page number here was taken from a later edition of Hutchinson's work than the one cited in other footnotes in the present study. See the Lawrence S. Mayo edition (Cambridge, Mass.: Harvard University Press, 1936).

Promised Land," Cotton Mather wrote in a volume describing the state of New England at the time of the witchcraft difficulties, "is all over fill'd with Fiery flying serpents. . . . All our way to Heaven, lies by the Dens of Lions, and the Mounts of Leopards; there are incredible Droves of Devils in our way." [70] We will return to discussion of this wilderness theme at the conclusion of the chapter, but for the moment it is important to note that Massachusetts had lost much of its concern for institutions and policies and had begun to seek some vision of its future by looking into a ghostly, invisible world.

It was while the people of the colony were preoccupied with these matters that the witches decided to strike.

I

No one really knows how the witchcraft hysteria began, but it originated in the home of the Reverend Samuel Parris, minister of the local church. In early 1692, several girls from the neighborhood began to spend their afternoons in the Parris' kitchen with a slave named Tituba, and it was not long before a mysterious sorority of girls, aged between nine and twenty, became regular visitors to the parsonage. We can only speculate what was going on behind the kitchen door, but we know that Tituba had been brought to Massachusetts from Barbados and enjoyed a reputation in the neighborhood for her skills in the magic arts. As the girls grew closer together, a remarkable change seemed to come over them: perhaps it is not true, as someone later reported, that they went out into the forest to celebrate their own version of a black mass, but it is apparent that they began to live in a state of high tension and shared secrets with one another which were hardly becoming to quiet Puritan maidens.

[70] Cotton Mather, "Wonders of the Invisible World," Boston and London, 1693, found in Samuel G. Drake, editor, *The Witchcraft Delusion in New England* (Roxbury, Mass.: W. Elliot Woodward, 1866), pp. 80–81.

Before the end of winter, the two youngest girls in the group succumbed to the shrill pitch of their amusements and began to exhibit a most unusual malady. They would scream unaccountably, fall into grotesque convulsions, and sometimes scamper along on their hands and knees making noises like the barking of a dog. No sooner had word gone around about this extraordinary affliction than it began to spread like a contagious disease. All over the community young girls were groveling on the ground in a panic of fear and excitement, and while some of the less credulous townspeople were tempted to reach for their belts in the hopes of strapping a little modesty into them, the rest could only stand by in helpless horror as the girls suffered their torments.

The town's one physician did what he could to stem the epidemic, but he soon exhausted his meagre store of remedies and was forced to conclude that the problem lay outside the province of medicine. The Devil had come to Salem Village, he announced; the girls were bewitched. At this disturbing news, ministers from many of the neighboring parishes came to consult with their colleague and offer what advice they might. Among the first to arrive was a thoughtful clergyman named Deodat Lawson, and he had been in town no more than a few hours when he happened upon a frightening exhibition of the devil's handiwork. "In the beginning of the evening," he later recounted of his first day in the village,

I went to give Mr. Parris a visit. When I was there, his kinswoman, Abigail Williams, (about 12 years of age,) had a grievous fit; she was at first hurried with violence to and fro in the room, (though Mrs. Ingersoll endeavored to hold her,) sometimes making as if she would fly, stretching up her arms as high as she could, and crying "whish, whish, whish!" several times. . . . After that, she run to the fire, and began to throw fire brands about the house; and run against the back, as if she would run up the chimney, and, as they said, she had attempted to go into the fire in other fits.[71]

[71] Deodat Lawson, "A Brief and True Narrative of Witchcraft at Salem Village," 1692, in *Narratives of the Witchcraft Cases, 1648–1706,* edited by George Lincoln Burr (New York: Scribner's, 1914), p. 154.

Faced by such clear-cut evidence, the ministers quickly agreed that Satan's new challenge would have to be met with vigorous action, and this meant that the afflicted girls would have to identify the witches who were harassing them.

It is hard to guess what the girls were experiencing during those early days of the commotion. They attracted attention everywhere they went and exercised a degree of power over the adult community which would have been exhilarating under the sanest of circumstances. But whatever else was going on in those young minds, the thought seems to have gradually occurred to the girls that they were indeed bewitched, and after they had been coaxed over and over again to name their tormentors, they finally singled out three women in the village and accused them of witchcraft.

Three better candidates could not have been found if all the gossips in New England had met to make the nominations. The first, understandably, was Tituba herself, a woman who had grown up among the rich colors and imaginative legends of Barbados and who was probably acquainted with some form of voodoo. The second, Sarah Good, was a proper hag of a witch if Salem Village had ever seen one. With a pipe clenched in her leathery face she wandered around the countryside neglecting her children and begging from others, and on more than one occasion the old crone had been overheard muttering threats against her neighbors when she was in an unusually sour humor. Sarah Osburne, the third suspect, had a higher social standing than either of her alleged accomplices, but she had been involved in a local scandal a year or two earlier when a man moved into her house some months before becoming her husband.

A preliminary hearing was set at once to decide whether the three accused women should be held for trial. The girls were ushered to the front row of the meeting house, where they took full advantage of the space afforded them by rolling around in apparent agony whenever some personal fancy (or the invisible agents of the devil) provoked them to it. It was a remarkable show. Strange creatures flew about the room pecking at the girls or taunting them from the rafters, and it was immediately obvious to everyone that the women on trial were responsible for all the disorder and suffering. When Sarah Good and Sarah Osburne were called to the stand and asked why they sent these spectres to torment the girls, they were too appalled to say much in their defense. But when Tituba took the stand she had a ready answer. A lifetime spent in bondage is poor training for standing up before a bench of magistrates, and anyway Tituba was an excitable woman who had breathed the warmer winds of the Caribbean and knew things about magic her crusty old judges would never learn. Whatever the reason, Tituba gave her audience one of the most exuberant confessions ever recorded in a New England courtroom. She spoke of the creatures who inhabit the invisible world, the dark rituals which bind them together in the service of Satan; and before she had ended her astonishing recital she had convinced everyone in Salem Village that the problem was far worse than they had dared imagine. For Tituba not only implicated Sarah Good and Sarah Osburne in her own confession but announced that many other people in the colony were engaged in the devil's conspiracy against the Bay.

So the hearing that was supposed to bring a speedy end to the affair only stirred up a hidden hornet's nest, and now the girls were urged to identify other suspects and locate new sources of trouble. Already the girls had become more than unfortunate victims: in the eyes of the community they were diviners, prophets, oracles, mediums, for only they could see the terrible spectres swarming over the countryside and tell what persons had sent them on their evil errands. As they became caught up in the enthusiasm of their new work, then, the girls began to reach into every corner of the community in a search for likely suspects. Martha Corey was an upstanding woman in the village whose main mistake was to snort incredulously at the girls' behavior. Dorcas Good, five years old, was a daughter of the accused Sarah. Rebecca Nurse was a saintly old woman who had been bedridden at the time of the earlier hearings. Mary Esty and Sarah Cloyce were Rebecca's younger sisters, themselves accused when they rose in energetic defense of the older woman. And so it went—John Proctor, Giles Corey, Abigail Hobbs, Bridgit Bishop, Sarah Wild, Susanna Martin, Dorcas Hoar, the Reverend George Burroughs: as winter turned into spring the list of suspects grew to enormous length and the Salem jail was choked with people awaiting trial. We know nothing about conditions of life in prison, but it is easy to imagine the tensions which must have echoed within those grey walls. Some of the prisoners had cried out against their relatives and friends in a desperate effort to divert attention from themselves, others were witless persons with scarcely a clue as to what had happened to them, and a few (very few, as it turned out) were accepting their lot with quiet dignity. If we imagine Sarah Good sitting next to Rebecca Nurse and lighting her rancid pipe or Tituba sharing views on supernatural phenomena with the Reverend George Burroughs, we may have a rough picture of life in those crowded quarters.

By this time the hysteria had spread well beyond the confines of Salem Village, and as it grew in scope so did the appetites of the young girls. They now began to accuse persons they had never seen from places they had never visited (in the course of which some absurd mistakes were made),[72] yet their word was so little questioned that it was ordinarily warrant enough to put respected people in chains.

From as far away as Charlestown, Nathaniel Cary heard that his wife had been accused of witchcraft and immediately traveled with her to Salem "to see if the afflicted did know her."

[72] John Alden later reported in his account of the affair that the girls pointed their fingers at the wrong man when they first accused him of witchcraft and only realized their mistake when an obliging passer-by corrected them. See Robert Calef, "More Wonders of the Invisible World," Boston, 1701, in Burr, *Narratives,* p. 353.

The two of them sat through an entire day of hearings, after which Cary reported:

I observed that the afflicted were two girls of about ten years old, and about two or three others, of about eighteen. . . . The prisoners were called in one by one, and as they came in were cried out of. . . . The prisoner was placed about seven or eight feet from the Justices, and the accusers between the Justices and them; the prisoner was ordered to stand right before the Justices, with an officer appointed to hold each hand, lest they should therewith afflict them, and the prisoner's eyes must be constantly on the Justices; for if they looked on the afflicted, they would either fall into their fits, or cry out of being hurt by them. . . . Then the Justices said to the accusers, "which of you will go and touch the prisoner at the bar?" Then the most courageous would adventure, but before they had made three steps would ordinarily fall down as in a fit. The Justices ordered that they should be taken up and carried to the prisoner, that she might touch them; and as soon as they were touched by the accused, the Justices would say "they are well," before I could discern any alteration. . . . Thus far I was only as a spectator, my wife also was there part of the time, but no notice taken of her by the afflicted, except once or twice they came to her and asked her name.

After this sorry performance the Carys retired to the local inn for dinner, but no sooner had they taken seats than a group of afflicted girls burst into the room and "began to tumble about like swine" at Mrs. Cary's feet, accusing her of being the cause of their miseries. Remarkably, the magistrates happened to be sitting in the adjoining room—"waiting for this," Cary later decided—and an impromptu hearing took place on the spot.

Being brought before the Justices, her chief accusers were two girls. My wife declared to the Justices that she never had any knowledge of them before that day; she was forced to stand with her arms stretched out. I did request that I might hold one of her hands, but it was denied me; then she desired me to wipe the tears from her eyes, and the sweat from her face, which I did; then she desired she might lean herself on me, saying she should faint. Justice Hathorne replied, she had strength enough to torment those persons, and she should have strength enough to stand. I speaking something against their cruel proceedings, they commanded me to be silent, or else I should be turned out of the room. An Indian . . . was also brought in to be one of her accusers: being come in, he now (when before the Justices) fell down and tumbled about like a hog, but said nothing. The Justices asked the girls, "who afflicted the Indian?", they answered "she" (meaning my wife). . . . The Justices ordered her to touch him, in order of his cure . . . but the Indian took hold of her in a barbarous manner; then his hand was taken off, and her hand put on his, and the cure was quickly wrought. . . . Then her mittimus was writ.[73]

For another example of how the hearings were going, we might listen for a moment to the examination of Mrs. John Proctor. This record was taken down by the Reverend Samuel Parris himself, and the notes in parentheses are his. Ann Putnam and Abigail Williams were two of the most energetic of the young accusers.

JUSTICE: Ann Putnam, doth this woman hurt you?

PUTNAM: Yes, sir, a good many times. (Then the accused looked upon them and they fell into fits.)

JUSTICE: She does not bring the book to you, does she? [74]

PUTNAM: Yes, sir, often, and saith she hath made her maid set her hand to it.

JUSTICE: Abigail Williams, does this woman hurt you?

WILLIAMS: Yes, sir, often.

JUSTICE: Does she bring the book to you?

WILLIAMS: Yes.

JUSTICE: What would she have you do with it?

WILLIAMS: To write in it and I shall be well.

PUTNAM TO MRS. PROCTOR: Did you not tell me that your maid had written?

MRS. PROCTOR: Dear child, it is not so. There is another judgment, dear child. (Then Abigail and Ann had fits. By and by they cried out, "look you, there is Goody Proctor upon the beam." By and by both of them cried out of Goodman Proctor himself, and said

[73] Reproduced in Calef, "More Wonders," in Burr, *Narratives,* pp. 350–352.

[74] The "book" refers to the Devil's registry. The girls were presumably being tormented because they refused to sign the book and ally themselves with Satan.

he was a wizard. Immediately, many, if not all of the bewitched, had grievous fits.)

JUSTICE: Ann Putnam, who hurt you?

PUTNAM: Goodman Proctor and his wife too. (Some of the afflicted cried, "there is Proctor going to take up Mrs. Pope's feet—and her feet were immediately taken up.)

JUSTICE: What do you say Goodman Proctor to these things?

PROCTOR: I know not. I am innocent.

WILLIAMS: There is Goodman Proctor going to Mrs. Pope (and immediately said Pope fell into a fit).

JUSTICE: You see, the Devil will deceive you. The children could see what you was going to do before the woman was hurt. I would advise you to repentance, for the devil is bringing you out.[75]

This was the kind of evidence the magistrates were collecting in readiness for the trials; and it was none too soon, for the prisons were crowded with suspects. In June the newly arrived Governor of the Bay, Sir William Phips, appointed a special court of Oyer and Terminer to hear the growing number of witchcraft cases pending, and the new bench went immediately to work. Before the month was over, six women had been hanged from the gallows in Salem. And still the accused poured in.

As the court settled down to business, however, a note of uncertainty began to flicker across the minds of several thoughtful persons in the colony. To begin with, the net of accusation was beginning to spread out in wider arcs, reaching not only across the surface of the country but up the social ladder as well, so that a number of influential people were now among those in the overflowing prisons. Nathaniel Cary was an important citizen of Charlestown, and other men of equal rank (including the almost legendary Captain John Alden) were being caught up in the widening circle of panic and fear. Slowly but surely, a faint glimmer of skepticism was introduced into the situation; and while it was not to assert a modifying influence on the behavior of the court for some time to come, this new

[75] Hutchinson, *History,* II, pp. 27–28.

voice had became a part of the turbulent New England climate of 1692.

Meantime, the girls continued to exercise their extraordinary powers. Between sessions of the court, they were invited to visit the town of Andover and help the local inhabitants flush out whatever witches might still remain at large among them. Handicapped as they were by not knowing anyone in town, the girls nonetheless managed to identify more than fifty witches in the space of a few hours. Forty warrants were signed on the spot, and the arrest total only stopped at that number because the local Justice of the Peace simply laid down his pen and refused to go on with the frightening charade any longer—at which point, predictably, he became a suspect himself.

Yet the judges worked hard to keep pace with their young representatives in the field. In early August five persons went to the gallows in Salem. A month later fifteen more were tried and condemned, of which eight were hung promptly and the others spared because they were presumably ready to confess their sins and turn state's evidence. Nineteen people had been executed, seven more condemned, and one pressed to death under a pile of rocks for standing mute at his trial. At least two more persons had died in prison, bringing the number of deaths to twenty-two. And in all that time, not one suspect brought before the court had been acquitted.

At the end of this strenuous period of justice, the whole witchcraft mania began to fade. For one thing, the people of the Bay had been shocked into a mood of sober reflection by the deaths of so many persons. For another, the afflicted girls had obviously not learned very much from their experience in Andover and were beginning to display an ambition which far exceeded their credit. It was bad enough that they should accuse the likes of John Alden and Nathaniel Cary, but when they brought up the name of Samuel Willard, who doubled as pastor of Boston's First Church and President of Harvard College, the magistrates flatly told them they were mistaken. Not long afterwards, a brazen finger was pointed directly at the executive mansion in Boston, where Lady Phips awaited her husband's return from an expedition to Canada, and one tradition even has it that Cotton Mather's mother was eventually accused.[76]

This was enough to stretch even a Puritan's boundless credulity. One by one the leading men of the Bay began to reconsider the whole question and ask aloud whether the evidence accepted in witchcraft hearings was really suited to the emergency at hand. It was obvious that people were being condemned on the testimony of a few excited girls, and responsible minds in the community were troubled by the thought that the girls' excitement may have been poorly diagnosed in the first place. Suppose the girls were directly possessed by the devil and not touched by intermediate witches? Suppose they were simply out of their wits altogether? Suppose, in fact, they were lying? In any of these events the rules of evidence used in court would have to be reviewed—and quickly.

Deciding what kinds of evidence were admissible in witchcraft cases was a thorny business at best. When the court of Oyer and Terminer had first met, a few ground rules had been established to govern the unusual situation which did not entirely conform to ordinary Puritan standards of trial procedure. In the first place, the scriptural rule that two eye-witnesses were necessary for conviction in capital cases was modified to read that any two witnesses were sufficient even if they were testifying about different events—on the interesting ground that witchcraft was a "habitual" crime. That is, if one witness testified that he had seen Susanna Martin bewitch a horse in 1660 and another testified that she had broken uninvited into his dreams twenty years later, then both were witnesses to the same general offense. More important, however, the court accepted as an operating principle the old idea that Satan could not assume the shape of an innocent person, which meant in effect that any

[76] Burr, *Narratives*, p. 377.

spectres floating into view which resembled one of the defendants must be acting under his direct instruction. If an afflicted
young girl "saw" John Proctor's image crouched on the window
sill with a wicked expression on his face, for example, there
could be no question that Proctor himself had placed it there,
for the devil could not borrow that disguise without the permission of its owner. During an early hearing, one of the defendants had been asked: "How comes your appearance to hurt
these [girls]?" "How do I know," she had answered testily, "He
that appeared in the shape of Samuel, a glorified saint, may appear in anyone's shape." [77] Now this was no idle retort, for every
man who read his Bible knew that the Witch of Endor had once
caused the image of Samuel to appear before Saul, and this
scriptural evidence that the devil might indeed be able to im-
personate an innocent person proved a difficult matter for the
court to handle. Had the defendant been able to win her point,
the whole machinery of the court might have fallen in pieces
at the magistrates' feet; for if the dreadful spectres haunting the
girls were no more than free-lance apparitions sent out by the
devil, then the court would have no prosecution case at all.

All in all, five separate kinds of evidence had been admitted
by the court during its first round of hearings. First were trials
by test, of which repeating the Lord's Prayer, a feat presumed
impossible for witches to perform, and curing fits by touch were
the most often used. Second was the testimony of persons who
attributed their own misfortunes to the sorcery of a neighbor on
trial. Third were physical marks like warts, moles, scars, or any
other imperfection through which the devil might have sucked
his gruesome quota of blood. Fourth was spectral evidence, of
the sort just noted; and fifth were the confessions of the accused
themselves.

Now it was completely obvious to the men who began to

[77] Cotton Mather, "Wonders of the Invisible World," in Drake, *The
Witchcraft Delusion,* p. 176.

review the court's proceedings that the first three types of evidence were quite inconclusive. After all, anyone might make a mistake reciting the Lord's Prayer, particularly if the floor was covered with screaming, convulsive girls, and it did not make much sense to execute a person because he had spiteful neighbors or a mark upon his body. By those standards, half the people in Massachusetts might qualify for the gallows. This left spectral evidence and confessions. As for the latter, the court could hardly maintain that any real attention had been given to that form of evidence, since none of the executed witches had confessed and none of the many confessors had been executed. Far from establishing guilt, a well-phrased and tearfully delivered confession was clearly the best guarantee against hanging. So the case lay with spectral evidence, and legal opinion in the Bay was slowly leaning toward the theory that this form of evidence, too, was worthless.

In October, Governor Phips took note of the growing doubts by dismissing the special court of Oyer and Terminer and releasing several suspects from prison. The tide had begun to turn, but still there were 150 persons in custody and some 200 others who had been accused.

In December, finally, Phips appointed a new session of the Superior Court of Judicature to try the remaining suspects, and this time the magistrates were agreed that spectral evidence would be admitted only in marginal cases. Fifty-two persons were brought to trial during the next month, and of these, forty-nine were immediately acquitted. Three others were condemned ("two of which," a contemporary observer noted, "were the most senseless and ignorant creatures that could be found"),[78] and in addition death warrants were signed for five persons who had been condemned earlier. Governor Phips responded to these carefully reasoned judgments by signing reprieves for all eight of the defendants anyway, and at this, the court began to empty

[78] Calef, "More Wonders," in Burr, *Narratives,* p. 382.

the jails as fast as it could hear cases. Finally Phips ended the costly procedure by discharging every prisoner in the colony and issuing a general pardon to all persons still under suspicion.

The witchcraft hysteria had been completely checked within a year of the day it first appeared in Salem Village.

II

Historically, there is nothing unique in the fact that Massachusetts Bay should have put people on trial for witchcraft. As the historian Kittredge has pointed out, the whole story should be seen "not as an abnormal outbreak of fanaticism, not as an isolated tragedy, but as a mere incident, a brief and transitory episode in the biography of a terrible, but perfectly natural, superstition." [79]

The idea of witchcraft, of course, is as old as history; but the concept of a malevolent witch who makes a compact with Satan and rejects God did not appear in Europe until the middle of the fourteenth century and does not seem to have made a serious impression on England until well into the sixteenth. The most comprehensive study of English witchcraft, for example, opens with the year 1558, the first year of Elizabeth's reign, and gives only passing attention to events occurring before that date.[80]

In many ways, witchcraft was brought into England on the same current of change that introduced the Protestant Reformation, and it continued to draw nourishment from the intermittent religious quarrels which broke out during the next century and a half. Perhaps no other form of crime in history has been a better index to social disruption and change, for outbreaks of

[79] George L. Kittredge, *Witchcraft in Old and New England* (New York: Russell E. Russell, 1956), p. 329.

[80] Wallace Notestein, *History of Witchcraft in England* (Washington, D.C.: The American Historical Society, 1911).

witchcraft mania have generally taken place in societies which are experiencing a shift of religious focus—societies, we would say, confronting a relocation of boundaries. Throughout the Elizabethan and early Stuart periods, at any rate, while England was trying to establish a national church and to anchor it in the middle of the violent tides which were sweeping over the rest of Europe, increasing attention was devoted to the subject. Elizabeth herself introduced legislation to clarify the laws dealing with witchcraft, and James I, before becoming King of England, wrote a textbook on demonology which became a standard reference for years to come.

But it was during the Civil Wars in England that the witchcraft hysteria struck with full force. Many hundreds, probably thousands of witches were burned or hung between the time the Civil Wars began and Oliver Cromwell emerged as the strong man of the Commonwealth, and no sooner had the mania subsided in England than it broke out all over again in Scotland during the first days of the Restoration. Every important crisis during those years seemed to be punctuated by a rash of witchcraft cases. England did not record its last execution for witchcraft until 1712, but the urgent witch hunts of the Civil War period were never repeated.

With this background in mind, we should not be surprised that New England, too, should experience a moment of panic; but it is rather curious that this moment should have arrived so late in the century.

During the troubled years in England when countless witches were burned at the stake or hung from the gallows, Massachusetts Bay showed but mild concern over the whole matter. In 1647 a witch was executed in Connecticut, and one year later another woman met the same fate in Massachusetts.[81] In 1651 the General Court took note of the witchcraft crisis in England and published an almost laconic order that "a day of hu-

---

[81] Winthrop, Journal, II, pp. 323, 344–345. Altogether, five or possibly six persons were executed for witchcraft in New England prior to the outbreak of 1692.

miliation" be observed throughout the Bay,[82] but beyond this, the waves of excitement which were sweeping over the mother country seemed not to reach across the Atlantic at all. There was no shortage of accusations, to be sure, no shortage of the kind of gossip which in other days would send good men and women to their lonely grave, but the magistrates of the colony did not act as if a state of emergency was at hand and thus did not declare a crime wave to be in motion. In 1672, for example, a curious man named John Broadstreet was presented to the Essex County Court for "having familiarity with the devil," yet when he admitted the charge the court was so little impressed that he was fined for telling a lie.[83] And in 1674, when Christopher Brown came before the same court to testify that he had been dealing with Satan, the magistrates flatly dismissed him on the grounds that his confession seemed "inconsistent with truth." [84]

So New England remained relatively calm during the worst of the troubles in England, yet suddenly erupted into a terrible violence long after England lay exhausted from its earlier exertions.

In many important respects, 1692 marked the end of the Puritan experiment in Massachusetts, not only because the original charter had been revoked or because a Royal Governor had been chosen by the King or even because the old political order had collapsed in a tired heap. The Puritan experiment ended in 1692, rather, because the sense of mission which had sustained it from the beginning no longer existed in any recognizable form, and thus the people of the Bay were left with few stable points of reference to help them remember who they were. When they

[82] Massachusetts Records, IVa, pp. 52–53.
[83] Essex County Records, I, p. 265.
[84] Essex County Records, V, pp. 426–427.

looked back on their own history, the settlers had to conclude that the trajectory of the past pointed in quite a different direction than the one they now found themselves taking: they were no longer participants in a great adventure, no longer residents of a "city upon a hill," no longer members of that special revolutionary elite who were destined to bend the course of history according to God's own word. They were only themselves, living alone in a remote corner of the world, and this seemed a modest end for a crusade which had begun with such high expectations.

In the first place, as we have seen, the people of the colony had always pictured themselves as actors in an international movement, yet by the end of the century they had lost many of their most meaningful contacts with the rest of the world. The Puritan movement in England had scattered into a number of separate sects, each of which had been gradually absorbed into the freer climate of a new regime, and elsewhere in Europe the Protestant Reformation had lost much of its momentum without achieving half the goals set for it. And as a result, the colonists had lost touch with the background against which they had learned to assess their own stature and to survey their own place in the world.

In the second place, the original settlers had measured their achievements on a yardstick which no longer seemed to have the same sharp relevance. New England had been built by people who believed that God personally supervised every flicker of life on earth according to a plan beyond human comprehension, and in undertaking the expedition to America they were placing themselves entirely in God's hands. These were men whose doctrine prepared them to accept defeat gracefully, whose sense of piety depended upon an occasional moment of failure, hardship, even tragedy. Yet by the end of the century, the Puritan planters could look around them and count an impressive number of accomplishments. Here was no record of erratic providence; here was a record of solid human enterprise, and with this realization, as Daniel Boorstin suggests, the settlers moved from a "sense of mystery" to a "consciousness of mastery," [85] from a helpless reliance on fate to a firm confidence in their own abilities. This shift helped clear the way for the appearance of the shrewd, practical, self-reliant Yankee as a figure in American history, but in the meantime it left the third generation of settlers with no clear definition of the status they held as the chosen children of God.

In the third place, Massachusetts had been founded as a lonely pocket of civilization in the midst of a howling wilderness, and as we have seen, this idea remained one of the most important themes of Puritan imagery long after the underbrush had been cut away and the wild animals killed. The settlers had lost sight of their local frontiers, not only in the sense that colonization had spread beyond the Berkshires into what is now upper state New York, but also in the sense that the wilderness which had held the community together by pressing in on it from all sides was disappearing. The original settlers had landed in a wilderness full of "wild beasts and wilder men"; yet sixty years later, sitting many miles from the nearest frontier in the prosperous seaboard town of Boston, Cotton Mather and other survivors of the old order still imagined that they were living in a wilderness—a territory they had explored as thoroughly as any frontiersmen. But the character of this wilderness was unlike anything the first settlers had ever seen, for its dense forests had become a jungle of mythical beasts and its skies were thick with flying spirits. In a sense, the Puritan community had helped mark its location in space by keeping close watch on the wilderness surrounding it on all sides; and now that the visible traces of that wilderness had receded out of sight, the settlers invented a new one by finding the shapes of the forest in the middle of the community itself.[86]

And as the wilderness took on this new character, it seemed

[85] Daniel Boorstin, *The Genius of American Politics* (Chicago: University of Chicago Press, 1953).

[86] See, again, the very interesting paper "Puritanism, The Wilderness and the Frontier" by Heimert.

that even the Devil had given up his more familiar disguises. He no longer lurked in the underbrush, for most of it had been cut away; he no longer assumed the shape of hostile Indians, for most of them had retreated inland for the moment; he no longer sent waves of heretics to trouble the Bay, for most of them lived quietly under the protection of toleration; he no longer appeared in the armies of the Counter-Reformation, for the old battlefields were still and too far away to excite the imagination. But his presence was felt everywhere, and when the colonists began to look for his new hiding places they found him crouched in the very heart of the Puritan colony. Quite literally, the people of the Bay began to see ghosts, and soon the boundaries of the New England Way closed in on a space full of demons and incubi, spectres and evil spirits, as the settlers tried to find a new sense of their own identity among the landmarks of a strange, invisible world. Cotton Mather, who knew every disguise in the Devil's wardrobe, offered a frightening catalogue of the Devil's attempts to destroy New England.

I believe, there never was a poor Plantation, more pursued by the wrath of the Devil, than our poor New-England. . . . It was a rousing alarm to the Devil, when a great Company of English Protestants and Puritans, came to erect Evangelical Churches, in a corner of the world, where he had reign'd without control for many ages; and it is a vexing Eye-sore to the Devil, that our Lord Christ should be known, and own'd and preached in this howling wilderness. Wherefore he has left no Stone unturned, that so he might undermine his Plantation, and force us out of our Country.

First, the Indian Powawes, used all their Sorceries to molest the first Planters here; but God said unto them, Touch them not! Then, Seducing spirits came to root in this Vineyard, but God so rated them off, that they have not prevail'd much farther than the edges of our Land. After this, we have had a continual blast upon some of our principal Grain, annually diminishing a vast part of our ordinary Food. Herewithal, wasting Sicknesses, especially Burning and Mortal Agues, have Shot the Arrows of Death in at our Windows. Next, we have had many Adversaries of our own Language, who have been perpetually assaying to deprive us of those English Liberties, in the encouragement whereof these Territories have been settled. As if this had not been enough; the Tawnies among whom we came have watered our Soil with the Blood of many Hundreds of Inhabitants. . . . Besides all which, now at last the Devils are (if I may so speak) in Person come down upon us with such a Wrath, as is justly much, and will quickly be more, the Astonishment of the World.[87]

And this last adventure of the Devil has a quality all its own.

Wherefore the Devil is now making one Attempt more upon us; an Attempt more Difficult, more Surprising, more snarl'd with unintelligible Circumstances than any that we have hitherto Encountered. . . . An Army of Devils is horribly broke in upon the place which is the center, and after a sort, the First-born of our English Settlements: and the Houses of the Good People there are fill'd with the doleful shrieks of their Children and Servants, Tormented by Invisible Hands, with Tortures altogether preternatural.[88]

The witchcraft hysteria occupied but a brief moment in the history of the Bay. The first actors to take part in it were a group of excited girls and a few of the less savory figures who drifted around the edges of the community, but the speed with which the other people of the Bay gathered to witness the encounter and accept an active role in it, not to mention the quality of the other persons who were eventually drawn into this vortex of activity, serves as an index to the gravity of the issues involved. For a few years, at least, the settlers of Massachusetts were alone in the world, bewildered by the loss of their old destiny but not yet aware of their new one, and during this fateful interval they tried to discover some image of themselves by listening to a chorus of voices which whispered to them from the depths of an invisible wilderness.

[87] Cotton Mather, "Wonders of the Invisible World," in Drake, *The Witchcraft Delusion,* pp. 94–95.
[88] *Ibid.,* pp. 16–17.

4

Stabilities and Instabilities
in Puritan Crime Rates

ALTHOUGH the chapter just concluded has taken up fully half the space in this book, it covers but one of the three general points mentioned in Chapter 1. In order to avoid any confusion on this point, it might be well to review the original plan of the study. It will be remembered that the first chapter included a fairly long essay on the subject of deviant behavior and then outlined three "implications" of that essay which were supposed to provide the underlying framework for the rest of the book. Chapter 3 discussed the relationship between a community's boundaries and the kinds of deviation likely to be encountered. The present chapter, however, represents a rather abrupt change of pace, not only because it is addressed to a different topic but also because it is concerned with a different kind of data. The following pages will turn to the second theme suggested in the introductory section—that the volume of deviance found in a community is likely to remain constant over time.

In the first chapter (to which the reader may want to refer again before continuing) it was proposed that social groups are likely to experience a relatively stable "quota" of deviation, partly because their social control machinery is calibrated to handle a steady flow of deviant conduct and partly because a group's definition of deviant behavior is usually phrased in such a way as to embrace a given segment of its range of experience (see pages 23 through 27). The purpose of the present chapter, then, is to see whether this highly speculative hypothesis is of any value in helping us understand something about Puritan crime rates in Massachusetts Bay. It should be clear by now that the term "hypothesis" is being used in its most general sense throughout the study—as a tentative supposition provisionally adopted in the hopes that it will explain certain facts and guide in the investigation of others. Our assignment here is not to "test" the supposition but to see if it makes any sense when exposed to the light of actual human experience.

In earlier portions of the study we dealt with the same sort of material historians use to reconstruct the past, but in the present chapter we will be consulting a somewhat different order of data: we will examine the records of the Essex County Court and enumerate the items listed there in an attempt to compute crime rates for this one section of the country.

It is here that the distinction mentioned earlier between the "particular" interests of the historian and the "general" interests of the sociologist may have some application. When a student is primarily concerned with learning how a given society developed or changed from one period to the next, he naturally looks at those pivotal events which seem to "make" history— decisive battles, important shifts of national mood, the appearance of new ideologies and new technologies. But when the student is primarily concerned with the underlying structures of society he must look for his data in the ordinary cycles of everyday life, in the habits and behavior of everyday people, for these point to a dimension of history which can only be learned by observing how often commonplace events reoccur. In the following pages, then, we will be dealing with hundreds of unknown settlers who appeared in the courtrooms of Essex County just long enough to become a statistic in the colony's records. Few of these appearances mean much in themselves, but together they tell us something about deviant behavior in colonial New England—and, hopefully, about deviant behavior everywhere.

The Essex County Court sat for the first time in 1636 as one of four inferior courts established in Massachusetts Bay to absorb the overflow of the busy Court of Assistants. Although these lower tribunals were specifically prohibited from dealing with crimes punishable by death, banishment, or the removal of a limb, their jurisdiction in criminal cases was otherwise rather ambiguous, and it was not at all uncommon during the first years of the new judicial arrangement for both higher and lower courts to hear actions of the same kind. In 1643 this situation was partly clarified when the colony was divided into four shires or counties, each with its own local court, and it became the usual practice for criminal actions to originate at the county level. As late as 1644, however, the Court of Assistants was still dealing with minor offenses like petty larceny and drunkenness which could have been handled in the county courts, although the number of such cases had dropped off considerably.[1] In 1649, it was expressly ordered that the higher court could not exercise original jurisdiction over cases triable in the county courts, and from that date the Court of Assistants limited its interest in criminal matters to cases of a major kind and cases on appeal from the county courts.

From the early 1650's until 1682 (the last date for which records have survived) the Essex County Court was the main agency for dealing with deviant behavior in the northeast corner of Massachusetts. For the purposes of the present analysis, we will assume that these records provide a *complete coverage of all deviant activities in the county*. While this assumption is not apt to be true in any literal sense, the paragraphs to follow will

[1] Massachusetts Records, II, pp. 138–139.

review some of the reasons why it is nonetheless a plausible one for Essex County in the seventeenth century.

When one argues that a single set of court records contains virtually every instance of deviant behavior in a given region, one is assuming two things: first, that the court in question was practically the only agency in the region with authority to "do something" about deviance, and second, that almost all persons defined as deviant in the region were brought before it. Now it is quite obvious that neither of these assumptions would be accurate in most parts of the contemporary world, since courts of law are but one of several agencies equipped to deal with deviant behavior and since large numbers of deviancies are handled at some informal level of control without becoming registered in any kind of official record. But the strict orthodoxy of the Massachusetts colony and its stern emphasis on community discipline combine to offer a historical case in which both of these conditions seem to hold.

The first assumption, then, is that the Essex County Court exersized such broad jurisdiction over errant behavior that its records include practically every act of deviation committed by a resident of the county. The Court of Assistants, to be sure, had original jurisdiction over all capital offenses and a number of other serious crimes, and furthermore several smaller courts were created during the century to hear cases of minor importance; but there is good reason to think that the number of actions tried in these courts remained small.

Although records of the Court of Assistants are not intact for the period covered in this study, the fragments which remain offer a few helpful hints as to the number of Essex County residents who appeared before it. To begin with, the surviving records list only twenty-nine criminal offenses for the entire period between 1642 and 1673.[2] This figure may be wholly meaningless, of course, because we do not know what proportion of

[2] Massachusetts Records, III, index.

the original cases are represented by this sample, but even if the actual number were four times greater, it would still be true that Essex County, with roughly 25 per cent of the colony's population, would be responsible for no more than one case per year. The records of the Court of Assistants are complete, however, for the period 1673 to 1692, and these figures allow us to make a better informed estimate of the matter. Some ninety-seven criminal actions were heard during that twenty-year period,[3] and if we take into account that the population of the colony had increased considerably by that time, it is reasonable to guess that something in the neighborhood of one hundred actions were heard in the thirty-year period preceding it, of which twenty-five or so would have been referred from Essex County—again, about one per year. Add to this that many if not most of these cases would have been on appeal from earlier actions of the county court, and we can feel secure that few deviants from Essex County were processed by the Court of Assistants without first leaving their mark in the local records.

The several courts which operated below the county level present less of a problem, for they were essentially designed to hear small claims and to expedite the business of strangers passing through the locality. On those occasions when the Commissioners' and Strangers' Courts did try offenders for misdemeanors of one sort or another, furthermore, the fact was ordinarily noted in the minutes of the county court and is thus included in the figures of the study.

A third category of courts might be mentioned in passing. Each church in the colony had authority to try members of its own congregation for various forms of delinquency, but the presence of these ecclesiastical tribunals does little to invalidate the assumption. In the first place, church courts exersized dual jurisdiction with civil courts, so that in ordinary circumstances a person would only be tried in church after he had been dealt with

[3] Massachusetts Records, I, index.

by civil authority, as we saw in the case of Anne Hutchinson. In the second place, some solid information is available about these church trials and it suggests that they were seldom used during the seventeenth century. Emil Oberholzer, who did a thorough study of church records throughout the colony, found that only twenty-nine offenses were brought to trial in the churches of Essex for the entire period from 1630 to 1689.[4]

The Essex County Court convicted 1369 persons of 2382 offenses between 1641 and 1682. Even if we make generous allowances about the number of persons from the county who might have been given a deviant label elsewhere, we would still have to conclude that the local court record is virtually a complete registry of deviant activities which came to official notice.

The second assumption we must deal with is that the county court was the central clearing house for all forms of deviant behavior, including those not ordinarily considered "crime," and that the community in general acted to bring deviancies to public attention rather than handling them in some more informal fashion. As we shall see in the final chapter, the Puritans of the Bay viewed deviant behavior with a straightforward logic that did not permit many subtle shadings between various forms of misbehavior. In a given day, for instance, the court might take notice of persons who drank too much, who were "without the use of their reason," who lived a scandalous life, who dressed in inappropriate clothes or let their hair grow too long, who swore, bragged, or talked too much, who disobeyed their parents or engaged in frivolous games. The saints did not appreciate the distinction invented by later generations between persons who infringe the customs of the group and persons who flatly violate the law, for the Word of God governed everything and had to be protected with all the machinery at the state's

---

[4] Emil Oberholzer, Jr., *Delinquent Saints: Disciplinary Actions in the Early Congressional Churches of Massachusetts* (New York: Columbia University Press, 1956).

disposal. The court's responsibility, then, extended to every mode of behavior which might offend in the eyes of God. For example:

It is further ordered, that no person, householder or other, shall spend his time idly or unprofitably, under pain of such punishment as the Court shall think meet to inflict; and for this end it is ordered, that the constable of every place shall use special care and diligence to take knowledge of offenders of this kind, especially of common coasters, unprofitable fowlers, and tobacco takers.[5]

Francis Usselton fined for cursing a swine of Henry Haggett, "a pox o' God upon her and the Devil take her." [6]

Court being informed that John Haverill lay in a house by himself contrary to the law of the country, whereby he is subject to much sin and iniquity, which ordinarily are the companions of a solitary life, it is ordered . . . that within six weeks after date he remove and settle himself in some orderly family in the town, and be subject to the orderly rules of family government, . . . which if he refuses, a warrant shall place him in the house of correction at Hampton.[7]

Joseph Swett's wife fined ten shillings for wearing a silk hood.[8]

And so on.

Not only did the jurisdiction of the court range over a wide assortment of deviancies, but the community in general was by no means reluctant to bring these deviancies to the court's attention. In our own day, many people who are considered deviant within the circle of their own family or their own neighborhood never appear in public records because "something is done about them" at a less formal level of control, but this was not typically the case in the Bay colony. Puritan discipline was largely a matter of community vigilance, and each citizen, no matter what his official function in the control apparatus, was expected to guard the public peace as carefully as he would the

[5] Essex County Records, I, p. 109.
[6] Essex County Records, II, p. 50.
[7] Essex County Records, V, p. 104.
[8] Essex County Records, I, p. 303.

peace of his own household. This meant that he had license to watch over his neighbors or even to spy on them, to inquire about their business or disrupt their privacy, so long as his main purpose was to protect the morality of the community. Nathaniel Hawthorne described Massachusetts Bay as a place "where iniquity was dragged out into the sunshine," and it was regarded the sternest duty of a citizen to do his part in this moral housecleaning. Sometimes, it would seem, this obligation was taken so earnestly that even the magistrates were taken aback:

One ——————, a godly minister, upon conscience of his oath and care of the commonwealth, discovered to the magistrates some seditious speeches of his own son, delivered in private to himself; but the court thought it not fit to call the party in question then, being loathe to have the father come in as a public accuser of his own son, but rather desired to find another matter, or other witnesses against him.[9]

On the whole, then, we may conclude that almost every voice in the colony contributed something to the social control apparatus and that fewer deviants slipped through this network without attracting public attention than is the case in most modern communities. The towns were small and compact, the congregations watchful; every person was tuned to the movements of his neighbor. In an atmosphere as tightly disciplined as this, it would be small wonder that people were sensitive to each others' affairs and ready to interfere when any hint of sin or scandal threatened. One student of social life in the colony wrote:

The people of the community knew each other's virtues, weaknesses, habits. Every woman in town could tell just how many gowns Goodwife Collins had in her chest, just how many dishes in her kitchen, how many feather beds she inherited from her father, and shook her head when word went around that she had lost her temper when the cow kicked over the milk.[10]

[9] Winthrop, Journal, I, p. 126.
[10] Thomas J. Wertenbaker, *The Puritan Oligarchy* (New York: Grosset and Dunlap, 1947).

Needless to add, any greater irregularities in Goodwife Collins' behavior were very apt to bring her trembling into court, where her neighbors, secure in the knowledge that they were doing their duty both to her and to the Lord, would recite her delinquencies into the public record.

The records of the Essex County Court have been printed in a seven volume set for the years 1636 to 1682. Although no absolute guarantees can be made about this kind of historical material, the records are generally thought to be complete.[11]

The analyses which follow are based upon a careful count of all criminal actions brought before the court from the beginning of 1651 (a date selected because the local court had by that time established a clear jurisdiction of its own) until the end of 1680. Each conviction entered into the record has been placed into one of the following groups:

1. Crimes against the church (disturbing the congregation, absence from church, contempt of the ministry, and so on).

2. Contempt of authority (criticism of the government, contempt of court, abusing public officials).

3. Fornication (including offenses charged against married parents who delivered their first child within too short a period after the wedding).

4. Disturbing the peace (drunkenness, disorderly conduct, and so on).

5. Crimes against property (largely a matter of theft).

6. Crimes against persons (assault, slander, defamation).

7. Other.

This last grouping includes convictions for unknown offenses (an item often overlooked in Puritan court reporting) and convic-

[11] Essex County Records. See footnote 34, p. 118, for full citation.

tions for crimes which took place too infrequently to be listed in separate categories.

Because the purpose of this study is to observe broad shifts over a fairly long span of years, the data have been grouped into six periods of five years each: thus we will be comparing the number of offenses recorded between 1651 and 1655 with the number recorded between 1656 and 1660, and so on. This procedure will make it difficult for us to keep track of smaller fluctuations in the various rates, of course, but it will make the larger shifts all the more visible.

As one can easily imagine, the data reported here have to be understood as very rough and approximate. Appendix I at the end of the study outlines some of the problems which have come up in trying to organize this material into more precise categories, but for the moment it is important to appreciate (1) that the data themselves are subject to all the error one might expect in records three hundred years old; and (2) that further error very likely occurred in the process of translating these seventeenth-century scraps of information into twentieth-century tables. For these reasons, the analyses which follow are based only on findings which seem so evident that no one could reasonably attribute them to the ragged condition of the data themselves.

In most of the following tables and graphs, enumerations will be expressed as incidence rates per 100 of the population. It should be borne in mind that these rates are figured for five-year periods rather than the more usual one, which means that they cannot be directly compared to most modern estimates of the incidence of crime. The population estimates used in these calculations are again rough and have been reported in Appendix II at the end of the study.

Table 1 shows the number of convictions recorded in the Essex County Court for the period 1651 to 1680:

TABLE 1

	1651–1655	1656–1660	1661–1665	1666–1670	1671–1675	1676–1680
Convictions	190	275	394	393	391	311
Population	4500	5200	6100	7300	8900	7500
Per 100 population	4.22	5.29	6.46	5.38	4.38	4.15

It is immediately evident that the number of convictions rose considerably near the middle of the thirty-year period and reached its lowest ebbs at the beginning and at the end—hardly supporting the hypothesis of stability with which this section of the study is concerned. But when we compare this "conviction rate" with another set of figures which might for present purposes be called the "offender rate," we see far greater evidence of the stability we are looking for:

TABLE 2

	1651–1655	1656–1660	1661–1665	1666–1670	1671–1675	1676–1680
Offenders	161	182	222	257	324	269
Population	4500	5200	6100	7300	8900	7500
Per 100 population	3.60	3.50	3.64	3.52	3.64	3.58

The "offender rate" reported in this table was computed by adding together all persons actively engaged in deviant behavior during each of the five-year periods, disregarding the number of convictions entered against a particular person's name. Thus a person guilty of two offenses in his life, one taking place in 1653 and the other in 1657, would be considered an "active offender" in both of the first two periods, while a person who committed twelve crimes between 1652 and 1655 would only be counted once in that period.

When the "conviction rate" and the "offender rate" are plotted on a graph (see Figure 1) the difference between them appears striking: clearly, the number of persons engaged in one or another form of deviant behavior remains fairly constant despite the fact that the number of offenses they manage to accumulate soars pyramidlike in the middle of the period and drops off considerably toward its end. Rather than comment on this finding now, however, we will turn to another table and look at the incidence rates for each given category of offense. (Because of the small numbers involved, crimes against property and crimes against persons have been combined. The figures in the table, remember, represent the number of offenses in each category per 100 of the population.)

There are two points of interest in these data which deserve a special word of comment.

It is apparent that the proportion of offenses which falls into the "other" category remains large throughout the thirty-year period, testifying to the difficulties of drawing exact information from such vintage records. It is interesting to note that the county court was highly selective in its omissions: although there were several hundred instances during the period in which the court recorder failed to mention the nature of the

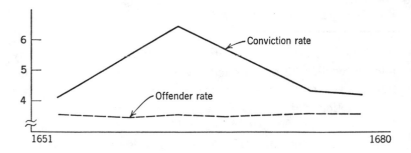

Figure 1

TABLE 3

	1651–1655	1656–1660	1661–1665	1666–1670	1671–1675	1676–1680
Crimes against the church	0.36	1.85	3.15	1.86	0.67	0.32
Contempt of authority	0.80	0.92	0.89	1.19	1.25	0.76
Fornication	0.78	0.62	0.44	0.51	0.85	1.02
Disturbing the peace	0.13	0.25	0.30	0.44	0.28	0.27
Persons, property	0.87	0.77	1.02	0.89	0.75	0.92
Other	1.29	0.88	0.67	0.49	0.58	0.84
	4.23 *	5.29	6.47 *	5.38	4.38	4.13 *

* Rounding error

offense being tried, only once did he neglect to mention the name of the defendant and never the sentence of the court. It is difficult to guess what this means. Perhaps the Puritans were simply less concerned with the formal definition of a person's transgression than with the stark fact that he had sinned against the community; perhaps the charges read in court were so vaguely worded that the recorder himself did not know what to write down (it is easy to imagine this problem arising in the trial of Anne Hutchinson, for example). But, in any case, the fact that one can only speculate about the nature of these omissions would suggest that we pay no special attention to smaller fluctuations in the rates, although it is intriguing to wonder why crimes against the church and fornication appear to vary inversely from one another.

There is one line of figures in the table, however, which would seem significant no matter how inexact the data, and this is the remarkable increase of crimes against the church in the middle of the thirty-year period. This bulge was created almost entirely by one of the three crime waves discussed earlier, for this was the interval during which the Quakers were most active in Essex County. In the previous chapter, we saw the Quakers foraging their noisy way across the colony and learned something about the exasperation of the magistrates as they tried to come to terms with the problem; but in the present chapter we are dealing with the flat statistics this group of people left behind them in the records of the court.

Fifty-one persons appear in the Essex County Court records who can be presumed to have had Quaker sympathies, and this small company of men and women was responsible for some 383 convictions during the period covered by this study. These offenses can be summarized as follows:

TABLE 4

	1651–1655	1656–1660	1661–1665	1666–1670	1671–1675	1676–1680
Crimes against the church	0	86	171	101	4	2
Contempt of authority	2	1	3	0	0	0
Disturbing the peace	0	1	8	2	0	0
Theft	0	0	1	0	0	0
Other	0	1	0	0	0	0

The figures in Table 4 make it apparent that the great increase of convictions in the middle of the thirty-year period is wholly due to the presence of the Quakers; in fact, the total conviction rate would even be a little depressed during those critical years if the Quaker offenses were taken from it (Table 5).

These figures show to better advantage when plotted on a graph (see Figure 2).

TABLE 5

	1651–1655	1656–1660	1661–1665	1666–1670	1671–1675	1676–1680
Conviction rate	4.22	5.29	6.46	5.38	4.38	4.15
Same, less Quaker convictions	4.18	3.58	3.46	3.97	4.35	4.12

When we make the same comparison with the offender rate, a curious fact begins to emerge. As we have seen, the number of persons actively involved in one or another form of deviation in each five-year period changed very little from one point in time to the next. This means that the fifty-one Quakers who entered the scene in the late 1650's were somehow absorbed into the deviant population without affecting its size to any appreciable extent, almost as if other potential offenders had withdrawn for the moment to make room for them (see Figure 3).

There are two possible explanations for this interesting finding. First, one might suspect that the fifty-one Quakers who crowded into the courtrooms of Essex County were predisposed to deviancy anyway and would have turned to another form of misbehavior if the new heresy had not drawn their attention. We know very little about these people, after all, and it is quite

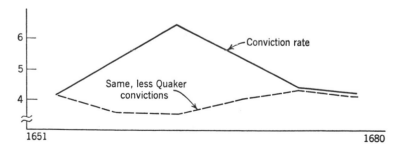

Figure 2

TABLE 6

	1651– 1655	1656– 1660	1661– 1665	1666– 1670	1671– 1675	1676– 1680
Offender rate	3.60	3.50	3.64	3.52	3.64	3.58
Same, less Quaker offenders	3.56	2.63	2.89	3.14	3.61	3.56

possible that they only chose this particular mode of deviant expression because it had a certain glamour and timeliness or because it was so readily available to them. Yet it is important to observe that these fifty-one persons, for all their volitility and willingness to challenge authority, were responsible for very few offenses either before or after the Quaker crisis. In 1648, one of them was sentenced for an unspecified offense, but in the twelve-year period between 1641 and 1653 there is no other entry in the court record implicating one of the people who later became a Quaker, and in the period between 1676 and 1682 there are only two passing indications that any of the fifty-one heretics committed a further offense. This would seem to suggest that the Quakers were not very inclined toward other forms of deviation and would not have appeared in court at all if the religious

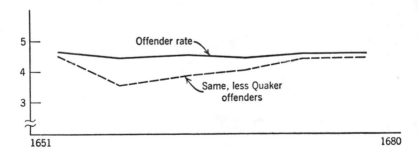

Figure 3

circumstances had been different. The second possible explanation, then, is that the Quakers were drawn into the deviant enclave by a shift in the political climate and in a sense replaced a number of people who might otherwise have been there.

Perhaps the most compelling reason for entertaining the second of these explanations is that the Quakers showed only the faintest attraction toward offenses not related to the religious struggle in which they were involved. The crimes they committed against the church (almost all of them a matter of absence from church services) were obviously of that character, and it is virtually certain that the convictions they received for disorderly conduct and contempt of authority were earned in the direct line of missionary duty. This leaves only an unexplained theft and one conviction in the "other" category.

When we mention the possibility that a handful of Quakers moved into the deviant ranks and displaced a number of people who were already there, we are of course speaking figuratively. We do not know what shifts and turns took place in the community during the Quaker crisis or what forces were at work to give the offender rate its distinctive shape. Yet the fact remains that this rate changed very little during the thirty-year period for which we have adequate records, suggesting that an almost fixed proportion of the populace was engaged in deviant activity before the Quakers made their abrupt appearance in the colony, during the time they were in full swing, and after they had retired from the field altogether. A crime wave lashed across Essex County which almost doubled the number of offenses handled by the local court, yet the size of the deviant population itself did not increase to any appreciable degree.

Now the many offenders who passed through the Essex County Court on their way to the whipping post and pillory were certainly not aware that they were contributing to a regular social pattern; yet somehow this odd scatter of individuals, acting without the slightest hint of collusion, managed to fashion that stable rate anyway. For the most part, social scientists are committed to the notion that regularities of this sort originate somewhere in the wider social structure, bringing order and predictability into peoples' activities whether they are aware of it or not, and a thorough sociological analysis of the problem would require us to turn our attention to those mechanisms in the social order which produce this stability. Unfortunately, however, we must bring this discussion of crime waves to an end just when we are ready to ask intelligent questions about them. We have been trying to tie a rather heavy theoretical package together with thin strands of evidence, and it would make better sense to postpone some of these important considerations until we can consult a more detailed set of data.

But in the meantime we can at least suggest where one might begin to look. We are dealing with a complicated problem of logistics here: while it is almost surely true that the number of deviants a society can afford to recognize has something to do with the capacity of its police force and of its courts, the relationship is by no means so easy as it may at first appear. The Essex County Court, for example, tried almost twice as many cases at the height of the Quaker crisis than it did before or after, and it is easy to imagine that the local constables were kept far busier during those frantic times than was their usual habit. Yet some kind of displacement was obviously taking place. Perhaps the courts were so alarmed by the Quaker invasion that they began to overlook matters which would otherwise have commanded their attention. Perhaps, alternatively, the presence of the Quakers created such a high volume of excitement and noise and drama that other potential offenders felt less disposed to enter the public arena with challenges against the conventional order. Whether we look for the source of this displacement in the capacity of the control apparatus, in the motives of the people involved, in the ever shifting definitions of deviance itself, or in some complex equation having to do with the density of deviant behavior in given units of social space, we are dealing with the notion that deviation in society may take the form of a distinct "quota."

For the moment we can only conclude that in one region of America, during one period of its history, the offender rate seems to have remained quite stable. If data from other communities show a similar pattern, we will have to consider the possibility that societies somehow "need" their quotas of deviation and function in such a way as to keep them intact.

5

Puritanism and Deviancy

I

IN January, 1636, a few weeks before the Antinomian controversy exploded over the colony of Massachusetts Bay, several ranking men of the community met together to discuss an important matter of policy. Henry Vane had just made a handsome entry into New England to take his place in the affairs of the Bay and was casting about for worthwhile issues to engage his attention. Among the rumors Vane heard as he measured the local political scene was that two of the most prominent men in the colony, John Winthrop and Thomas Dudley, were involved in a feud about discipline—the first preferring to act leniently in actions brought before the bench and the second committed to a policy of harsh Biblical justice. When Vane learned of the dispute he decided to offer his services as moderator. Accordingly, he and his recent travel companion, the Reverend Hugh Peters, invited several leaders of the community to join them in a discussion of the problem. As Winthrop relates the story (speaking of himself in the third person):

Mr. Vane and Mr. Peters, finding some distraction in the common-wealth, arising from some difference in judgment, and withal some alienation of affection among the magistrates and some other persons of quality, and that hereby factions began to grow among the people, some adhering more to the old governor, Mr. Winthrop, and others to the late governor, Mr. Dudley,—the former carrying matters with more lenity, and the latter with more severity,—they procured a meeting in Boston. . . .

The meeting itself opened rather hesitantly. Vane began by reciting his reasons for inviting the group to assemble, and then had to sit in awkward silence while first Winthrop and then Dudley flatly stated that they "knew not of any breach" between them and had only attended the conference to hear others "utter their own complaints." After a long and uncomfortable pause, Vane was finally rescued by John Haynes who offered to make a few remarks on the subject at issue. Winthrop, he complained, acted "too remissly in point of justice" and did not prosecute deviant offenders with the vigor expected of a Puritan magistrate. The old Governor replied that

it was his judgment, that in the infancy of a plantation, justice should be administered with more lenity than in a settled state, because people were then more apt to transgress, party of ignorance of new laws and orders, partly through oppression of business and other straits; but, if it might be made clear to him, that it was an error, he would be ready to take up a stricter course.

After further discussion of the matter it was decided that conventional Puritan protocol should be invoked, and so several ministers were asked to "set a rule" for the issue at hand. Next morning, when the conference reconvened, the clergymen announced their opinion—"that strict discipline, both in criminal and martial affairs, were more needful in plantations than in a settled state, as tending to the honor and safety of the gospel." Winthrop accepted this ruling with his usual courtesy and the meeting ended with "a renewal of love amongst them." [1]

[1] Winthrop, Journal, I, pp. 169–172.

This meeting has been cited by historians as one of the most significant turning points in the early history of the Bay because it set the judiciary on a course of severity which lasted for several generations. Yet the conference is important for another reason: it supplies us with one of our most revealing views of the way the settlers thought about deviant behavior and its control.

When Winthrop urged leniency in the administration of law he was speaking the language of practical political science, arguing that discipline should be scaled according to the nature of the situation. When the clergy reacted against this line of reasoning, however, they were speaking the language of sheer religious absolutism: discipline cannot be molded to fit the shifting circumstances of the time but must remain fixed and ultimate to protect the universal law of morality, the honor and safety of the gospel. "Crook not God's rules to the experience of men," one Puritan divine had written, "but bring them unto the rule, and try men's estates herein by that." [2] Thus, at the very moment England was learning to regard the law as a product of human experience, Massachusetts reaffirmed the old medieval conviction that law is a permanent set of standards written into the design of the universe and wholly unmoved by changes in the human condition.

Any discussion of Puritan attitudes toward deviancy and punishment should begin with an understanding of this essential position, for it suggests that crimes against the public order are crimes against the symmetry and orderliness of nature itself.

One of the most durable memories we have of old Massachusetts Bay is that the magistrates could be very cruel in their treatment of offenders, burning ugly brands into their flesh,

[2] Quoted in Miller, *The New England Mind: The Seventeenth Century,* p. 20.

turning them out into the wilderness, shaming them in the stocks and pillory, flogging them with a heavy hand, severing their ears and mutilating their noses, and sometimes even hanging them from the gallows. Students of American history have long been attracted to this grisly subject, not only the school children who learn something about Roger Williams and the witchcraft frenzy but whole generations of serious scholars as well. Until late in the nineteenth century (and even well into the twentieth) historians of Massachusetts wrote so much about Puritan severity that one might have thought they were postponing other relevant topics until they could come to terms with at least this one compelling chapter of the past. Some of these historians were looking for ways to exonerate the settlers of the Bay; others appeared to feel an urgent sense of outrage over the atrocities they thought they were reporting. Occasionally a writer like Nathaniel Hawthorne might draw an understanding portrait of the time without trying to take sides in those long dead disputes, but such men were easily outnumbered by the partisan observers around them —loyal apologists like John Palfrey or furious critics like James Truslow Adams.

Now historiography has come a long way since the nineteenth century and it would be absurd for us to be concerned because these writers did not observe modern conventions about neutrality in the study of the past. But even if we make lavish allowances for the fact that styles of scholarship have changed, we still have to admit that much of the material left to us gives us a poor angle of vision on colonial attitudes toward deviation. This material tells us a good deal about the Puritan appetite for persecution but almost nothing about the Puritan cosmology which lay behind it.

The fact seems to be that the punishment of crime in early Massachusetts was in many ways less severe than in other parts of the contemporary world, and this makes it difficult to understand why the colony should have earned such a lasting reputation for harshness. Perhaps the most terrifying thing about punishment in Massachusetts Bay, after all, was not its fierceness but its cold righteousness. Even the most merciless persecutions in other parts of the world were characterized by a degree of human sentimentality, if only because the participants were moved by feelings like rage, pity, revenge, or fear, but in Massachusetts Bay, justice was governed by a relentless kind of certainty. Little attention was paid to the motives of the offender, the grief of the victim, the anger of the community, or any other human emotion: the whole process had a flat, mechanical tone because it dealt with the laws of nature rather than with the decisions of men.

In order to understand this feature of Puritan justice, one should begin with the doctrine of predestination as it appeared in New England thinking. According to the Puritan reading of the Bible, as we have seen, there were only two important classes of people on earth—those who had been elected to everlasting life and those who had been consigned forever to hell. These decisions, of course, had been made before the people affected by them were born, and nothing they did in the course of their lives would have any influence on the outcome; yet the New England Puritans assumed that most men would sooner or later give evidence as to whether they were chosen or not. Persons who had felt grace would be so touched by the experience that they would develop a new sense of responsibility toward the community and slowly move into positions of leadership; persons who remained in doubt would stay in the middle ranks of the community and pursue their honest callings until they learned more of their fate; persons who had reason to fear the worst would drift sullenly into the lower echelons of society, highly susceptible to deviant forms of behavior. Thus the social structure of the Kingdom of God closely resembled that of the English nation, and it was obvious to the dullest saint that confirmed deviants belonged in the lowest of these ranks. If a man acts contemptuously toward authority and violates the norms of the community, God will not suddenly turn in wrath and reassign him to hell; but it is safe to assume that anyone who behaves in that fashion has not experienced and will not experience grace. He is not, as the term once implied, a "graceful" man.

Given these premises, Puritan attitudes toward punishment had a fairly simple logic. If a culprit standing before the bench is scheduled to spend eternity in hell, it does not matter very much how severely the judges treat him, for all the hardships and sufferings in the world will be no more than a faint hint of the torments awaiting him in the hereafter. In the ecclesiastical courts of medieval Europe, felons were sometimes sentenced to burn at the stake in the theory that this would represent an apt introduction to the fires of hell, and this is not wholly unlike the implicit notion which seems to have governed the courtrooms of New England. It was God, not the magistrates, who had sentenced the offender to everlasting suffering, and if the magistrates lashed a few stripes on his back or printed his skin with a hot iron, they were only doing what God, in His infinite wisdom, had already decreed. In a sense, then, the punishment of culprits was not only a handy method for protecting the public peace; it was an act of fealty to God.

The doctrine of predestination is often criticized as one of the cruelest of theologies since it condemns people to hell before they have had a chance to demonstrate whether they merit this fate or not. But it is important to understand that predestination was not just an article of dogma invented by people with hard imaginations: it was a description of life as the saints lived it, a natural explanation of happenings in the real world. God, they knew, was sovereign in all things, not only in broad natural cycles like the movement of the stars or the change of seasons, but in the most ordinary details of everyday life as well. Yet a number of things were difficult to explain in this world where nothing was left to human will or random chance: why, for example, are some men more gifted than others, some born to higher estates, some more fortunate in their daily enterprises? Clearly, God wills it that way:

God Almighty, in his most holy and wise providence, hath so disposed of the condition of mankind, as in all times some must be rich and some poor, some high and eminent in power and dignities, others mean and in subjection.[3]

And so the notion of predestination took the two most evident "facts" of Puritan experience—the given knowledge that God governed the universe and the empirical observation that men differed from one another—and combined them with all the precision and economy of a scientific theory.

Now this was fatalism of a most exaggerated kind, but like so many tenets of Puritan theology it was seldom taken literally. It was necessary for the Puritans to feel that every movement of the universe was supervised directly by God, but it was also necessary for them to feel that people who infringe the rules of society were both morally and legally responsible for their own deviancies; and soon the Puritans developed the kind of legalistic solution for which their minds were so superbly trained. God, so the reasoning went, arranges every moment of human history in advance and regulates the affairs of men down to the smallest detail. Every act of man, then, whether it be a saintly deed or a frightful crime, has been fully preordained. Yet at the same time, God demands that each person *consent* to the future which has been chosen for him, so that he is always acting on the basis of his own volition in the very process of carrying out God's will. This is almost like saying that a man who finds himself falling from a tree will decide on the way down that this is what he really planned to do anyway, but it served the needs of New England theory well enough and was not a worse sophistry than many other strains of Puritan creed. From a legal point of view, then, the will of man stays wholly free and he accepts responsibility for whatever he does, not because he could have chosen to act otherwise but because he volunteered for this outcome in

[3] John Winthrop, "A Model of Christian Charity," *Winthrop Papers* (Boston: Massachusetts Historical Society, 1931), II, p. 282.

the first place. When one of the most gifted theorists in the colony tried to explain this tricky point, he could only assert a little lamely that God so organized the world that men "should act freely, and yet that they should accomplish His purposes by all their free actions." [4]

From a twentieth-century point of view, of course, there is a very clear contradiction in this notion of criminal responsibility.

On the one hand, the deviant is doing little more than following a script which absolutely requires him to perform whatever delinquencies he is later punished for, and thus he cannot really be "blamed" for his own misconduct—at least in the way we have since learned to use the term. In this respect, punishment in Massachusetts had an almost sacrificial quality: the culprit was asked to accept punishment not because he could have "helped" it in any reasonable sense but because the logic of the universe simply required it of him.

On the other hand, every offender who came before the bench did so as a free man, entirely responsible for his own actions. He could not plead that he had been forced into sin by God's decree or that he came from a deprived background or that he was a victim of circumstances or even that he did not know any better—for in the very beginning he had made a contract with God to be an unregenerate sinner. There may be a certain dignity in this idea, after all, because it gives every man credit for being the master of his own destiny, but this may have been small consolation to those who had to face the consequences of that ambiguity. As in our own day, the Puritans found it convenient to assume that every human action had a "cause" somewhere in the intricate machinery of nature, but this did not make them feel for a moment that the person on whom this cause had operated was any the less responsible for what he did.

There is no evidence that people in seventeenth-century New England saw any contradiction in this notion, but it is a

[4] Quoted in Miller, *The New England Mind*, p. 193.

source of continuing confusion to the later commentator. When one spends many hours in the company of old records, it becomes increasingly difficult to understand what the Puritans meant when they called someone "guilty" or what they hoped to accomplish by punishing him. A few examples might help illustrate the problem.

In 1638, a Dorothy Talbye was brought into court for murdering her child, a girl with the haunting and prophetic name "Difficult." Mrs. Talbye's behavior both before and during her trial suggests that she was by no means a competent person, even by the crude psychiatric standards of that day. Winthrop thought that she was motivated by "melancholy and spiritual delusions" and attributed her crime to the fact that she was "so possessed with Satan, that he persuaded her (by his delusions, which she listened to as revelations from God) to break the neck of her own child, that she might free it from future misery." Despite this clinical impression she was hung in Boston and an excellent sermon preached on the occasion. Winthrop reports that she acted in a very undignified manner at her execution, refusing to repent, tearing off her hood as she stood on the scaffold, requesting to be beheaded rather than hanged ("giving this reason, that it was less painful and less shameful"), and struggling to free herself as she swung from the end of the rope. Whatever else might be said about this unfortunate woman, she most certainly did not die gracefully.[5]

In 1666, a woman named Jane Flanders was brought before the Essex County Court for "telling lies" and for "making debate among neighbors and casting great reproaches on several." The court found her "so distempered in her head" that she was prohibited from giving testimony at the trial; but this disability did not prevent her from being sentenced to "ten stripes on lecture day."[6]

And Cotton Mather, who knew a good deal about the sub-

[5] Winthrop, Journal, I, pp. 282–283.
[6] Essex County Records, III, pp. 319–320.

ject, tells a story about one of the colony's first witches. Ann Cole had once been "a person of serious piety," he tells us, but one day she was "taken with very strange fits" and began to perform remarkable feats like speaking in Dutch, a language she presumably did not know. When her fits had abated, she admitted that she had made a covenant with the Devil and had sealed the bargain by permitting him to have "frequent carnal knowledge of her." It goes without saying that Mrs. Cole was promptly hanged, but it is Mather's description of the event which remains the most perplexing. "Upon this confession," he informs us, "the woman was executed, whereupon Ann Cole was happily delivered from the extraordinary troubles wherewith she had been exercised." [7] One is tempted to ask whether the judges had rid the community of a dangerous witch or had cured the lady of an annoying illness! And this is perhaps the main point: deviant behavior *was* a kind of illness, not an occasion for warmth or sympathy, to be sure, but an emergency condition which had to be treated with every resource at the community's disposal, whether or not the patient suffered any discomfort in the process.

This brings us to another curious feature of Puritan justice, the extraordinary efforts made by both magistrates and ministers to extract a formal expression of repentance from convicted felons. The main purpose of these expressions, of course, was to purge the person's soul and perhaps give him a chance to convince the rest of the community that he was not really a bad sort of fellow. Throughout the records we find any number of occasions in which the court softened its judgment upon receipt of a touching confession or an earnest promise of reform. But this is only half the story, for some of the most celebrated confessions in the history of the Bay, collected with meticulous care by people like Cotton Mather, were those uttered by doomed men on their last fateful walk to the gallows; and it is difficult

[7] Mather, *Magnalia,* II, pp. 448–449.

to understand why so much importance was attached to them. Surely the culprit was not going to change his fate by being contrite at the last moment, nor was there any chance that the gesture would improve his prospects in the hereafter. It is important to remember, however, that repentance is a public ceremony of admission as well as a private act of contrition. To repent is to agree that the moral standards of the community are right and that the sentence of the court is just. To repent is to say (a phrase the Puritans loved to repeat) that one has "sinned against his own conscience" and entirely understands why the community has to punish or even kill him. (In this, again, as in so many other respects, the newer Puritanism of the Soviet Union seems to parallel the older Puritanism of New England.)

And here the circularities of Puritan theory meet together in a peculiar finale. The deviant plunges into a life of sin, impelled by forces beyond his control; yet in the final moment he is able to make a certain sense out of this inexorable process when he *consents* to the destiny which spells his destruction and when he stands on the scaffold and testifies that the laws about to destroy him are altogether reasonable and fair. In a sense, then, the victim is asked to endorse the action of the court and to share in the judgment against him, to move back into the community as a witness to his own execution. If the whole affair sounds a little like ritual sacrifice, we may all the more easily understand another element which may have been present in the Puritan attitude toward repentance—that the people of the community, vaguely aware of the contradictions of their own doctrine, were somehow anxious for the condemned man to forgive them.

II

With this background in mind, we can return to a problem introduced in Chapter 1. As has been suggested in various portions of the study, deviant persons often supply an important service to society by patrolling the outer edges of group space and by providing a contrast which gives the rest of the community some sense of their own territorial identity. When one approaches this problem from a cross-cultural frame of reference, one must note that every society handles this matter differently: each has its own mechanisms for naming people to deviant positions and its own mechanisms for regulating the human traffic moving back and forth from its boundaries. In Chapter 1 these various arrangements were called "deployment patterns" and reference was made to several of them which appear frequently in the ethnological literature (see pages 27 to 29). Now the main reason it is important to see some difference between these deployment patterns is to point out that each society is exercising a cultural option when it develops a characteristic way of looking at deviant behavior and a characteristic set of machinery for controlling it, for the way in which this option is exercised has a profound effect both on the forms of deviancy a society experiences and on the kinds of people who come to exhibit it.

The final paragraphs of the study, then, will explore two notions—first, that the Puritans developed a deployment pattern which was uniquely suited to the theological climate in which they lived, and second, that the main outlines of that pattern are still reflected in many of our modern attitudes toward deviation.

To characterize the New England deployment pattern in a word, we may say (1) that the Puritans saw deviant behavior as the special property of a particular class of people who were more or less frozen into deviant attitudes; and (2) that they generally thought it best to handle the problem by locking these people into fairly permanent deviant roles. Puritan theories of human development began with the assumption that men do not change a great deal as they mature or are exposed to different life experiences, and in this sense the settlers of the Bay

had little faith in the promise that men might "reform" or over-
come any pronounced deviant leanings. A person's character, like
his social estate, is fixed by the preordained pattern of human
history, and if he should somehow indicate by his surly manners and delinquent ways that he is not a very promising candidate for conversion, the community was not apt to waste many
of its energies trying to change him or mend his character. In
a very real sense, he belonged to a deviant "class" and was not
expected to improve upon that condition.

   This does not mean that the Puritans gave up on every delinquent who came before the bench, but it does mean that they
recognized a clear line beyond which a deviant was simply considered "lost." When the Puritans admonished a person or fined
him, they may only have meant to restore him to his better
senses; but when they branded him on the forehead or otherwise mutilated his face they were marking him with the permanent emblem of his station in life and making it extremely difficult for him to resume a normal social role in the community.
To banish him meant almost the same thing: he might earn a
better reputation elsewhere, but in local records and in local
memories he would remain a deviant forever, a fate considered
far worse in the seventeenth century than is true in the twentieth. The same finality, of course, was present in the act of execution.

   Perhaps one might conclude, then, that the Puritan deployment pattern was based on the almost permanent exclusion of
a deviant class—a category of misfits who would normally be expected to engage in unacceptable activities and to oppose the
rest of the social order. Like the other patterns alluded to in the
first chapter, the Puritan system acted to stabilize the volume of
deviation appearing in community life; but unlike the other patterns it made very little allowance for people to move back and
forth from the community's boundaries. Once a person had been
branded with the mark of disreputability, either figuratively or
literally, his status in society had been fairly well stabilized, and

it was exceedingly difficult for him to impress others (not to mention himself) that he was suited for another social position. Perhaps it is from the Puritans that we borrowed the odd rhetorical habit of saying about someone, "he is an addict" or "he is a schizophrenic," almost as if we were talking about his occupation. In many ways, this is precisely what the Puritans did mean by such a phrase: to characterize a person as deviant was to describe his spiritual condition, his calling, his vocation, his state of grace.

The theological views which sustained this deployment pattern have largely disappeared from the religious life of the society, but the attitudes toward deviation which were implied in the pattern are still retained in many of the institutions we have built to process and confine deviant offenders. We are still apt to visualize deviant behavior as the product of a deep-seated characterological strain in the person who enacts it, rather than as the product of the situation in which it took place, and we are still apt to treat that person as if his whole being was somehow implicated in what is often no more than a passing deviant episode. It would take another book of comparable size to argue whether or not this outlook makes any sense from a scientific point of view, although it is certainly appropriate to note that many of the deviant activities which trouble the public consciousness seem to be fairly specific in respect to age—suggesting that quite a few of our most active deviants might simply settle down in adulthood if we were able to regard their excursions into nonconformity as a function of age rather than as a function of basic character. The logic which invites us to view juvenile offenders as apprentice criminals, for example, says a good deal more about the structure of our society than about the psychological inclinations of the young people involved.

But, in any case, the purpose of the present study is to inquire whether these views are historically related to the theological doctrines which the Puritans brought to America more than three hundred years ago. It would be impossible, of course, to review the development of American thinking about deviation over that long period of time, and in this sense the question must be left hanging in mid-air; but we might, as a kind of epilogue, look at one episode in our history which suggests how the attitudes of that earlier age have claimed the interest of later generations.

III

Shortly after the American revolution, a group of people in Philadelphia began a movement of penal reform that was soon to spread all over the world. These men, many of them Quakers, argued that convicted felons should be taken from the stocks and pillories which stood in almost every township and placed in private prison cells where they could reflect on their misspent lives and improve their spiritual condition. Dr. Benjamin Rush, an important spokesman for the group, expressed the need for this reform in terms which seem vaguely familiar to modern ears. Writing in 1787, he declared:

The reformation of a criminal can never be effected by a public punishment. . . . Experience proves, that public punishments have increased propensities to crimes. A man who has lost his self-respect at a whipping post, has nothing valuable to lose in society. Pain has begotten insensibility to the whip; and shame to infamy. Added to his old habits of vice, he probably feels a spirit of revenge against the whole community, whose laws have inflicted his punishment upon him, and hence he is stimulated to add to the number and enormity of his outrages upon society.[8]

Prisons had been used before this time to confine suspects awaiting trial, of course, and to hold persons like debtors who had not been convicted of any crime, but they had seldom been employed as a punishment for convicted felons; and in this sense

[8] Quoted in Harry Elmer Barnes and Negley K. Teeters, *New Horizons in Criminology* (New York: Prentice-Hall, 1943), p. 412.

the Philadelphia proposal was fairly unique. Not long after the new century began, two large penitentiaries were constructed in the United States which became models for almost every penal institution built either in this country or in Europe. The first of these, Eastern State Penitentiary in Philadelphia, was a product of Quaker thinking and planning. Architecturally, it was a powerful fortress of stone, gloomy and massive like a medieval castle, but inside a new idea of prison discipline was being developed: each convict was locked in a separate cell and confined there for the duration of his sentence, working at useful trades in the privacy of his room and exercising by himself in an isolated courtyard. The whole arrangement bore the stamp of Quaker theology, for the stated purpose of this solitary treatment was to give the inmate a chance to come to terms with his inner self and gain a more religious outlook for the future.

The second of these model prisons, established at Auburn, New York, reflected a rather different set of theories. Where the Philadelphia system stressed solitude and separate confinement, the Auburn system stressed congregate activities. Inmates slept in segregated cells but moved into workshops during the day and even outside the prison walls to work in tightly disciplined gangs, eating together in a common mess hall. In order to maintain order among this large company of men, the Auburn officials made liberal use of the whip and enforced a policy of absolute silence among the convicts.

No sooner had the two prisons admitted their first inmates than they began to receive visitors from all over the world, and shortly a brisk rivalry broke out between adherents of the two prison systems. Auburn could boast of a very modest cost per inmate, since prison labor brought in enough revenue to take care of most expenses—and even the prison buildings themselves proved easy to finance when Sing Sing Prison was built from the ground with convict labor provided by Auburn. The Philadelphia model, on the other hand, claimed to be more humane, since its cells were rarely opened and no corporal punishment was necessary to keep the inmates in line. Yet the major issue of debate revolved around the question as to whether Philadelphia or Auburn was better equipped to reduce the amount of recidivism among its charges, and in this debate we can hear echoes of an argument which had begun more than 150 years earlier when the Quakers first landed in America and met the Puritans of New England.

When Alexis de Tocqueville and Gustave de Beaumont visited this country in 1831, one of their most important projects —and indeed the official purpose of their journey—was to study and compare the rival prison systems. Their conclusion remains one of the keenest observations on the subject made then or at any time since:

The Philadelphia system, being that which produces the deepest impressions on the soul of the convict, must effect more reformation than that of Auburn. The latter, however, is perhaps more conformable to the habits of men in society, and on this account effects a greater number of reformations which might be called "legal," inasmuch as they produce the external fulfillment of social obligations. If this be so, the Philadelphia system produces more honest men, and that of New York more obedient citizens.[9]

In a sense, then, the two prison models represented different philosophies of punishment and different psychologies of crime. The Philadelphia system, with its emphasis on penitence and solitude, took its major tone from the Quaker feeling that the resources for conversion lay within every man and that even the meanest rogue could improve his religious estate if he were separated from evil influences and left in a position where his better nature could begin to assert itself. The Auburn model, however, was not shaped to so gentle a view of man. Here the keynote was discipline: the men were assembled in long grey ranks, forbidden to speak to one another, kept at heavy labor,

[9] Gustave de Beaumont and Alexis de Tocqueville, *On the Penitentiary System in the United States and Its Application to France,* trans. Francis Lieber (Philadelphia: Carey, Lea and Blanchard, 1833), pp. 59–60.

and subject to constant harassment from the guards—all of which mirrored the Puritan conviction that a reprobate spirit must be broken to the routines of a useful life because it cannot be truly redeemed. While Philadelphia provided a setting in which a man's natural grace could emerge, Auburn offered a setting in which his inherent wickedness could at least be curbed and bent to the needs of society.

During their tour of America, Tocqueville and Beaumont met Elam Lynds, an energetic adherent of the Auburn system and its first long-term warden. At one point in the interview Tocqueville asked Lynds: "Do you really believe in the reform of a great number of prisoners?" And Lynds replied:

We must understand each other; I do not believe in a *complete* reform, except with young delinquents. Nothing, in my opinion, is rarer than to see a convict of mature age become a religious and virtuous man. I do not put great faith in the sanctity of those who leave the prison; I do not believe that the counsels of the chaplain, or the meditations of the prisoner, make a good Christian of him. But my opinion is, that a great number of old convicts do not commit new crimes, and that they even become useful citizens, having learned in prison a useful art, and contracted habits of constant labor. This is the only reform I ever have expected to produce, and I believe it is the only one which society has the right to expect.[10]

Lynds explained to his visitors that he warmly encouraged the use of corporal punishment because the convict has to be "broken to the yoke of discipline" before his sullen disposition can be turned to more "conformable" modes of conduct. When the interview was over, Tocqueville commented in his journal: "During the whole of this conversation which, with intervals, lasted several hours, Mr. Elam Lynds came continually back to the idea that it was most important of all to break the prisoner into a state of *passive obedience*." [11]

[10] *Ibid.*, p. 202.
[11] Alexis de Tocqueville, *Journey to America*, trans. George Lawrence and ed. J. P. Mayer (New Haven: Yale University Press, 1959), pp. 26–27.

The judgment of later generations has been hard on Elam Lynds. The most comprehensive work on the history of American penology describes him as a man of "undeniable cruelty" and concludes that his "name goes down in penal history as a scourge." [12] Lynds may indeed have been a cruel man, but it is more important to note that the philosophy he practiced was deeply rooted in the New England where he was born and is altogether consistent with the Puritan attitude toward crime and punishment. Lynds regarded flogging a far kinder punishment than solitary confinement (a judgment, by the way, which the very humane Charles Dickens endorsed when he visited the Philadelphia prison about that time) [13] and it seems apparent that he became warden of Auburn and later of Sing Sing in an earnest effort to correct what he considered the enormous "abuses" of the Philadelphia approach. Seen against its Puritan background, Lynd's penal theory seems intelligent and perhaps even kindly. If we assume that a convict's soul is permanently depraved and that sin is an inevitable part of his personal endowment, it makes very little sense to think in terms of "reform" or "regeneration"; the best one can do for him is to contain his reprobate spirit, in much the same way that one tames the wilder instincts of animals, and mold him into a passive, compliant, dulled member of the social order. The object of prison discipline is not to *improve* his nature, since this cannot be accomplished with even the harshest therapies, but to harness it so completely that it cannot assert itself. Tocqueville and Beaumont appeared to understand this point very well in their discussion of the Auburn convict:

Perhaps, leaving the prison, he is not an honest man; but he has contracted honest habits. He was an idler; now he knows how to work. His ignorance prevented him from pursuing a useful occupation; now he knows how to read and write; and the trade which he has learned

[12] Barnes and Teeters, p. 521.
[13] Charles Dickens, *American Notes for General Circulation* (London: Chapman and Hall, 1842).

in the prison furnishes him the means of existence which formerly he had not. Without loving virtue, he may detest the crime of which he has suffered the cruel consequences; and if he is not more virtuous he has become at least more judicious; his morality is not honor, but interest. His religious faith is perhaps neither lively nor deep; but even supposing that religion has not touched his heart, his mind has contracted habits of order. . . . Finally, if he has not become in truth better, he is at least more obedient to the laws, and that is all which society has the right to demand.[14]

The outcome of the rivalry between the Philadelphia and Auburn systems can be seen in almost every part of the world, for it is one of the curiosities of history that Auburn should become the model for almost every maximum security prison built in America and that Philadelphia should become the model for most such institutions built in Europe.

There are many reasons for this strange development, of course, having to do with matters of architecture, labor supply, and the like; but one of these reasons may have been that the Auburn philosophy reflected a theory of human nature which was largely unique to America—or at least best represented in American institutions. Although Puritanism started as an international movement and left its imprint in many corners of the world, the peculiar ethos it generated took root mainly in the United States, and this heritage is still evident in many of the methods we use to handle deviant conduct. The Auburn approach still provides the guiding principle for all but a few experimental prisons in this country: the silent system is rarely enforced, prison labor no longer competes with free labor on the open market, new programs have been introduced to rehabilitate offenders, but the fundamental attitudes toward crime and punishment which sustained the Auburn plan continue to retain an important place in our thinking about the matter. Now, as then, we leave few return routes open to people who try to resume a normal social life after a period of time spent on the commu-

[14] Beaumont and Tocqueville, *On the Penitentiary System*, pp. 58–59.

nity's boundaries, because most of us feel that anyone who skids off into the more severe forms of aberrant expression is displaying a serious defect of character, a deep blemish which cannot easily be erased. We may learn to think of such people as "sick" rather than "reprobate," but a single logic governs both of these labels, for they imply that nothing less than an important change of heart, a spiritual conversion or a clinical cure, can eliminate that inner seed which leads one to behave in a deviant fashion.

To return to the subject of the epilogue, at any rate, it might be pointed out that the Auburn system has not been notably successful as a method for rehabilitation. Modern studies of prison life indicate that recidivism is very high among convicts and that the atmosphere of the prison itself contributes importantly to that process. This outcome, however, cannot be written off as a simple failure of American inventiveness, for in many ways it is a very apt representation of American attitudes toward deviation: people in this society do not expect much in the way of reform from those who are labeled "deviant." And this, historically, brings us back to the Puritans, for it is their image of deviation, their belief in the irreversibility of human nature, which may be reflected in that expectation.

Appendix

APPENDIX ONE

IN order to keep an accurate roster of convictions, a separate key-sort card was filed for each offender who appeared before the court with data about the nature of his offense and the outcome of his trial entered upon it. For the most part, transferring these scattered pieces of information from the original records to the cards did not pose any unusual difficulties, but every now and then problems emerged that had to be settled rather arbitrarily. The most persistent problems were related to the thousands of names found in the records. The Puritans did not observe any consistent rules of spelling, with the result that a single name might be written in a number of fashions—even by the person to whom it belonged. For example, a man named Francis Usselton made frequent appearances before the Essex County Court, and the records which note these visits spell his name in at least fourteen different ways. These eccentricities of spelling do not make a great deal of difference in Francis Usselton's case, since the name is distinct and unusual in any of its various forms, but throughout the records there were more difficult decisions to make—for example, whether the George Hampton who stole a chicken in 1649 is the same man as the George Hampden who was found drunk in 1651, or whether Edwin and Edward Batter are two different persons.

To complicate the matter even further, Puritans often passed a favorite Christian name from generation to generation and thus one can never be sure whether a father or his son is being cited in court. A certain John Brown was convicted of seven offenses between 1656 and 1681, a simple enough history to report until this item appears in the records for 1679: "John Brown, son of John Brown, chose John Brown, his grandfather, as his guardian." One way to resolve this dilemma is to notice that the seven offenses were clustered in two distinct groups with an interval of almost twenty years between them, which would tend to suggest that two different generations of Browns were involved. As we know from other sources, this was indeed the case. But this is by no means an infallible indicator. A man named Giles Corey is remembered in the Essex County Court for five different offenses, three taking place in the 1640's, and two in the 1670's. If we knew nothing else about the man, we might reasonably assume that more than one person went under that name; but poor Giles Corey later earned a place in history when he was pressed to death under a pile of rocks during the witchcraft hysteria of 1692–1693, and as a result of his hard-won prominence we know that all five offenses were indeed his.

The study has not observed any firm rules for dealing with this order of difficulty. In many cases, inspection of other available records such as birth and death notices helps distinguish one life-span from another, but on the whole a great deal was left to the judgment of the investigator and in the process a number of errors were most certainly made—which is one of the reasons why the study deals only with broad indices.

Two other procedural tactics have been adopted in the course of the study which might be mentioned at this point. When a person was brought before the bench and convicted of several offenses at once, only the most serious of them was entered on the key-sort card. Similarly, when an offender was given more than one punishment—for example, put into the stocks and required to pay a two shilling fine—only the more severe penalty was listed. Never was there any serious question which of the two was the most severe from a Puritan's point of view.

APPENDIX TWO

THE population estimates for Essex County used in Chapter 4 were based on an extraordinary piece of demographical detective work done more than a hundred years ago by Joseph B. Felt.[1] In a monograph published in 1845, Felt used an assortment of old records to estimate the population of the colony at various times throughout its early history. According to these figures, the population of Massachusetts Bay increased as follows:

1639	8,592
1654	16,026
1665	23,467
1673	35,644

If we compute an annual increment for each year falling between those dates, we can estimate the population at the midpoint of each of the five-year units used in the study. This procedure is a precarious one even under the best of circumstances, but there is one period of years in the span covered by the study

[1] Joseph B. Felt, "Statistics of Population in Massachusetts," *Collections of the American Statistical Association,* I (1845), pp. 121–214.

which is even more troublesome than the rest: in 1675, Massachusetts became involved in a bloody campaign against an army of Indians, since known as King Philip's War, and this long season of fighting cost the colony a considerable number of casualties— not only among the combatants but among the settlers of outlying towns. It is impossible to estimate what this did to the population of the colony as a whole, and in the figures which follow we have simply made a guess informed only by the knowledge that the war was an extremely destructive one. Estimates of the population of the colony, then, read as follows:

Midpoint of period	Estimate based on Felt (rounded)	Present estimate
1653	15,550	
1658	18,700	
1663	22,800	
1668	28,050	
1673	35,650	
1678		35,650

As these estimates show, the assumption has been made that losses sustained during King Philip's War momentarily checked the high growth rate of the Bay colony.

These figures give us estimates for the population as a whole but do not provide us with any estimates for Essex County specifically. As it happens, however, the General Court frequently taxed the various counties either for men or money, and by figuring the proportions of the levy for each region in the colony, we can determine what percentage of the total lived in Essex County. Needless to say, these figures only give us what the General Court *thought* the population was in each shire, for no census was ever taken, but they are our best clue to the matter. There were fourteen different levies made on the various towns of the colony between 1633 and 1645, and the average share for the towns of Essex County was 30 per cent. In 1645, the proportion was 29 per cent. In 1675 (the next levy for which records survive) this share had dwindled to 25 per cent and in

1685 it had dropped all the way to 18 per cent—probably reflecting the fact that Essex County had suffered many more casualties during the Indian wars than the rest of the colony proportionally. Our estimate has to take into account, then, that the relative population of Essex County declined gradually in the latter part of the century, corresponding to the rise of Boston as a commercial center, and dropped sharply after King Philip's War. Not only did Essex County lose many men of fighting age during the war itself, but a good part of the civilian population was killed in Indian raids or migrated to other parts of New England during the touchy ten-year peace which followed.

The estimates for Essex County, then, can be summarized as follows:

Midpoint of period	Colony estimate	Essex per cent	Essex population
1653	15,550	29%	4,500
1658	18,700	28%	5,200
1663	22,800	27%	6,100
1668	28,050	26%	7,300
1673	35,650	25%	8,900
1678	35,650	21%	7,500

BIBLIOGRAPHY

The following list of titles has been divided into two general sections. The first includes works which have been useful in formulating the sociological argument of the book (although several of these titles are not "sociological" in the stricter sense of the term) and the second includes works from which historical material has been drawn about Massachusetts in the seventeenth century.

I

Barnes, Harry Elmer, and Negley K. Teeters, *New Horizons in Criminology*. Englewood Cliffs, N.J.: Prentice-Hall, 1943.

Bok, Curtis, *Star Wormwood*. New York: Knopf, 1959.

Caillois, Roger, *Man and the Sacred* (trans. Meyer Barash). Glencoe, Ill.: The Free Press, 1959.

Cohen, Albert K., "The Study of Social Disorganization and Deviant Behavior," in Merton et al., editors, *Sociology Today*. New York: Basic Books, 1959.

Conrad, Joseph, *The Secret Agent*. New York: Doubleday Anchor, undated.

Dentler, Robert A., and Kai T. Erikson, "The Functions of Deviance in Groups," *Social Problems*, 7 (1959), pp. 98–107.

Durkheim, Emile, "Deux Lois de l'Évolution Penale," *L'Année Sociologique*, IV (1901), pp. 65–95.

——, *The Division of Labor in Society* (trans. George Simpson). Glencoe, Ill.: The Free Press, 1960.

——, *The Rules of Sociological Method* (trans. Sarah A. Solovay and John H. Meuller). Glencoe, Ill.: The Free Press, 1958.

Erikson, Erik H., *Childhood and Society*. New York: Norton, 1950.

Fielding, Henry, "An Inquiry into the Causes of the Late Increase of Robbers . . ." (London, 1751), found in William E. Henley, editor, *The Complete Works of Henry Fielding, Esq.* New York: Groscup and Sterling, 1902, Vol. XIII.

Fyvel, T. R., "The Teddy Boy International," *Encounter*, XVII (1961), pp. 17–31.

Garfinkel, Harold, "Successful Degradation Ceremonies," *American Journal of Sociology*, LXI (1956), pp. 420–424.

Goffman, Erving, *Asylums*. New York: Bobbs-Merrill, 1962.

Goldhamer, Herbert, and Andrew W. Marshall, *Psychoses and Civilization*. Glencoe, Ill.: The Free Press, 1953.

Halpern, Ben, "History, Sociology, and Contemporary Area Studies," *American Journal of Sociology*, 63 (1957), pp. 1–10.

Howard, John, *The State of the Prisons*. London: J. M. Dent and Sons, 1929.

Huxley, Aldous, *Prisons: The "Carceri" Etchings by G. B. Piranesi*. London: The Trianon Press, 1949.

Martel, Martin U., "Some Controversial Assumptions in Parsons' Approach to Social System Theory," *Alpha Kappa Deltan*, 29 (1959), pp. 53–63.

Mead, George Herbert, "The Psychology of Punitive Justice," *American Journal of Sociology*, 23 (1918), pp. 577–602.

Merton, Robert K., *Social Theory and Social Structure*, revised edition. Glencoe, Ill.: The Free Press, 1957.

Michaels, Jerome, and Mortimer J. Adler, *Crime, Law and Social Science*. New York: Harcourt, Brace and World, 1933.

Parsons, Talcott, *The Social System*. Glencoe, Ill.: The Free Press, 1951.

Pound, Roscoe, *Social Control Through Law*. New Haven, Conn.: Yale University Press, 1942.

Shaw, George Bernard, *The Crime of Imprisonment*. New York: Philosophical Library, 1946.

Sykes, Gresham M., *The Society of Captives*. Princeton, N.J.: Princeton University Press, 1958.

Thrupp, Sylvia, "History and Sociology: New Opportunities for Co-operation," *American Journal of Sociology*, 63 (1957), pp. 11–16.

II

Adams, Brooks, *The Emancipation of Massachusetts: The Dream and the Reality*, second edition. Boston: Houghton Mifflin, 1919.

Adams, Charles Francis, *Massachusetts, Its Historians and Its History*. Boston: Houghton Mifflin, 1893.

——, editor, *Antinomianism in the Colony of Massachusetts Bay, 1636–1638*. Boston: Publications of the Prince Society, 1894.

——, *Three Episodes of Massachusetts History*, 2 vols. Boston: Houghton Mifflin, 1903.

Andrews, Charles M., *The Colonial Period of American History*, Vol. I, New Haven: Yale University Press, 1934.

Battis, Emery, *Saints and Sectaries*. Chapel Hill, N.C.: University of North Carolina Press, 1962.

Bishop, George, *New England Judged by the Spirit of the Lord* (London, 1703). Reprinted Philadelphia: Thomas W. Stuckney, 1885.

Boorstin, Daniel J., *The Genius of American Politics*. Chicago: University of Chicago Press, 1953.

Bradford, William, *Of Plimouth Plantation* (edited Samual E. Morison). New York: Knopf, 1952.

Brattle, Thomas, "An Account of the Delusion Called Witchcraft Which Prevailed in New England" (letter dated October, 1692), *Collections of the Massachusetts Historical Society*, Vol. 5, Series I, 1798.

Bridenbaugh, Carl, *Cities in the Wilderness: The First Century of Urban Life in America*. New York: Ronald Press, 1938.

Brown, B. Katherine, "A Note on the Puritan Concept of Aristocracy," *Mississippi Valley Historical Review*, XLI (1954), pp. 105–112.

——, "Freemanship in Puritan Massachusetts," *American Historical Review*, LIX (1954), pp. 865–883.

Burr, George L., editor, *Narratives of the Witchcraft Cases, 1648–1706*. New York: Scribner's, 1914.

Chafee, Jr., Zechariah, editor, "Records of the Suffolk County Court, 1671–1680," *Publications of the Colonial Society of Massachusetts*, Vol. XXIX, 1933.

Clark, John, "Ill Newes from New-England . . ." (London, 1652),

Collections of the Massachusetts Historical Society, Vol. II, Fourth Series, 1854.

Dow, Charles Francis, editor, *Records and Files of the Quarterly Courts of Essex County, Massachusetts, 1636–1682*, 7 volumes. Salem, Mass.: The Essex Institute, variously dated.

Downing, Emmanuel, letter to James Ussher (1620), *Collections of the Massachusetts Historical Society*, Vol. II, Fourth Series (1854), pp. 120–121.

Ellis, George Edward, "The Puritan Commonwealth: Its Basis, Organization, and Administration; Its Contentions; Its Conflicts with Heretics," in Justin Winsor, editor, *The Memorial History of Boston*, Vol. I. Boston: James Osgood, 1880.

Felltham, Owen, "Resolves: Divine, Moral, Political" (1623), in Peter Ure, editor, *Seventeenth Century Prose*, Vol. II. London: Penguin Books, 1956.

Felt, Joseph B., "Statistics of Population in Massachusetts," *Collections of the American Statistical Association*, I (1845), pp. 121–214.

French, Allen, *Charles I and the Puritan Upheaval*. London: George Allen and Unwin, 1955.

George, Charles H., and Katherine George, *The Protestant Mind of the English Reformation, 1570–1640*. Princeton, N.J.: Princeton University Press, 1961.

Goebel, Jr., Julius, "King's Law and Local Custom in Seventeenth Century New England," *Columbia Law Review*, 31 (1954), pp. 416–448.

Haller, William, *The Rise of Puritanism*. New York: Columbia University Press, 1938.

——, *Liberty and Reformation in the Puritan Revolution*. New York: Columbia University Press, 1955.

Haskins, George L., *Law and Authority in Early Massachusetts*. New York: Macmillan, 1960.

Heimert, Alan, "Puritanism, The Wilderness, and the Frontier," *New England Quarterly*, 26 (1953), pp. 361–382.

Hull, John, *Diary, Transactions and Collections of the American Antiquarian Society*. Boston: Printed for the Society, 1857.

(Hutchinson, Anne), A Report of the Trial of Mrs. Anne Hutchinson before the Church in Boston, March, 1638, *Proceedings of the Massachusetts Historical Society*, Vol. IV, Second Series (1888), pp. 161–191.

Hutchinson, Thomas, *The History of the Colony of Massachusetts-Bay.* . . . Boston: Thomas and John Fleet, 1764.

——, *The History of the Province of Massachusetts-Bay.* Boston: Thomas and John Fleet, 1767.

——, *Papers, Collections of the Massachusetts Historical Society,* Vol. X, Second Series, 1843; and Vol. I, Third Series, 1846.

Johnson, Edward, *Wonder-working Providence of Sion's Saviour in New England* (London, 1654), edited J. Franklin Jameson. New York: Scribner's, 1910.

Josselyn, John, "An Account of Two Voyages to New-England," *Collections of the Massachusetts Historical Society,* Vol. III, Third Series (1833), pp. 211–354.

Kittredge, George L., *Witchcraft in Old and New England,* second edition. New York: Russell and Russell, 1956.

McIlwain, Charles H., editor, *The Political Works of James I.* Cambridge, Mass.: Harvard University Press, 1918.

Maclear, James F., " 'The Heart of New England Rent': The Mystical Element in Early Puritan History," *Mississippi Valley Historical Review,* XLII (1956), pp. 621–652.

Mather, Cotton, "The Wonders of the Invisible World" (Boston and London, 1693), in Samuel G. Drake, editor, *The Witchcraft Delusion in New England.* Roxbury, Mass.: W. Elliot Woodward, 1866.

——, *Magnalia Christi Americana, or The Ecclesiastical History of New England* (London, 1702), 2 vols. Hartford: Silas Andrus and Son, 1853.

Michaelson, Robert S., "Changes in the Puritan Concept of Calling or Vocation," *New England Quarterly,* 26 (1953), pp. 315–336.

Miller, Perry, *Orthodoxy In Massachusetts, 1630–1650.* Cambridge, Mass.: Harvard University Press, 1933.

——, *The New England Mind: The Seventeenth Century.* New York: Macmillan, 1939.

——, "Preparation for Salvation in Seventeenth Century New England," *Journal of the History of Ideas,* IV (1943), pp. 253–279.

——, *The New England Mind: From Colony to Province.* Cambridge, Mass.: Harvard University Press, 1953.

——, *Errand in the Wilderness.* Cambridge, Mass.: Harvard University Press, 1960.

Morgan, Edmund S., "The Case Against Anne Hutchinson," *New England Quarterly,* X (1937), pp. 635–649.

Morgan, Edmund S., *The Puritan Dilemma: The Story of John Winthrop*. Boston: Little, Brown, 1958.

Morison, Samuel E., *Builders of the Bay Colony*. Boston: Houghton Mifflin, 1930.

Noble, John, and John F. Cronin, editors, *Records of the Court of Assistants of the Colony of Massachusetts Bay, 1630–1692.* Boston: Published by the County of Suffolk, Vol. I, 1901; Vol. II, 1904; Vol. III, 1924.

Notestein, Wallace, *History of Witchcraft in England.* Washington, D.C.: American Historical Society, 1911.

Oberholzer, Jr., Emil, *Delinquent Saints: Disciplinary Actions in the Early Congregational Churches of Massachusetts.* New York: Columbia University Press, 1956.

Palfrey, John G., *A Compendious History of New England,* 4 vols. Boston: Houghton Mifflin, 1873.

Park, Charles E., "Puritans and Quakers," *New England Quarterly,* 27 (1954), pp. 53–74.

Parrington, Vernon J., *Main Currents in American Thought,* Vol. I. New York: Harcourt, Brace and World, 1954.

Perry, Ralph Barton, *Puritanism and Democracy.* New York: Vanguard Press, 1944.

Schneider, Herbert W., *The Puritan Mind.* New York: Holt, Rinehart and Winston, 1930.

Sewell, Samuel, *Diary* (edited by Mark van Doren). New York: Macy-Masius, 1927.

Shurtleff, Nathaniel B., editor, *Records of the Governor and Company of the Massachusetts Bay in New England,* 5 vols. Boston: Printed by order of the Massachusetts Legislature, 1853–54.

Simpson, Alan, *Puritanism in Old and New England.* Chicago: University of Chicago Press, 1955.

Smith, Joseph H., editor, *Colonial Justice in Western Massachusetts: The Pynchon Court Record.* Cambridge, Mass.: Harvard University Press, 1961.

Starkey, Marion L., *The Devil in Massachusetts.* New York: Knopf, 1949.

Swan, Bradford F., "Roger Williams and the Insane," *Rhode Island History,* 5 (1946), pp. 65–70.

Trefz, Edward K., "Satan as the Prince of Evil," *Boston Public Library Quarterly,* 7 (1955), pp. 3–21.

Trevelyan, G. M., *History of England* (Vol. II, The Tudors and the Stuart Era). New York: Doubleday Anchor, 1959.

Ward, Nathaniel, "The Simple Cobler of Aggawam" (London, 1647), in Perry Miller, editor, *The American Puritans*. New York: Doubleday Anchor, 1956.

Wertenbaker, Thomas J., *The Puritan Oligarchy*. New York: Grosset and Dunlap, 1947.

Wheelwright, John, *Papers* (edited Charles H. Bell). Boston: Publications of the Prince Society, 1876.

Winslow, Ola Elizabeth, *Meetinghouse Hill*. New York: Macmillan, 1952.

Winthrop, John, "A Model of Christian Charity," *Winthrop Papers*, Vol. II. Boston: The Massachusetts Historical Society, 1931, pp. 282–295.

———, "A Short Story of the Rise, Reign, and Ruin of the Antinomians, Familists and Libertines that Infected the Churches of New England" (London, 1644). Reprinted in C. F. Adams, *Antinomianism*, see above.

———, *History of New England* (edited James K. Hosmer), 2 vols. New York: Scribner's, 1908.

Woodhouse, A. S. P., *Puritanism and Liberty*. London: J. M. Dent and Sons, 1938.

Index

Adams, Brooks, 52, 113–114
Adams, Charles Francis, 51, 82
Adams, James Truslow, 188
Alden, John, 145, 148, 149
Antinomian Controversy, the, 21, 71–107, 108, 127, 129, 133, 185
Auburn Prison, 200–204

Barnes, Harry Elmer, 199, 203
Battis, Emery, 70
Beaumont, Gustave de, 201, 202, 203–204
Becker, Howard S., 6
Bellingham, Richard, 127
Birdwhistell, Ray L., xii
Bishop, Bridgit, 145
Bishop, George, 107, 109, 117–118, 119, 120, 124, 127
Blau, Peter M., xii
Body of Liberties, 62
Boorstin, Daniel, 156–157
Boundaries, defined, 9–10
   as historical element, 19–23, 68–70

Boundaries, as related to deviant behavior, 10–13
Bradstreet, Simon, 130
Brend, William, 117
Broadstreet, John, 155
Brosin, Henry W., xii–xiii
Brown, Christopher, 155
Brown, Katherine B., 60
Burroughs, George, 145

Cambridge Platform, 110
Cartwright, Thomas, 41
Cary, Nathaniel, 145–147, 148, 149
Chafee, Zechariah, Jr., 56
Charles I, 37, 45, 154
Charles II, 124, 131, 134, 138
Church of England, 39, 40–41
Civil Wars, The, 46, 110–111, 154
Clark, John, 112
Cloyce, Sarah, 145
Coddington, William, 125
Code of 1648, 58, 110
   debate over, 59–62
Cohen, Albert K., 18
Cole, Ann, 194
Commitment ceremonies, 15–16

Communities, as focal concept, 9–10
Congregationalism, origins in England, 39–43
   social theory, 61–62, 72–74
Conrad, Joseph, 20
Corey, Giles, 145, 210
Corey, Martha, 144
Cotton, John, 63, 109, 113
   role during Antinomian Controversy, 75–76, 78–80, 85, 90–91, 96–97, 98, 102–104
Covenant of Grace, 83–87
Covenant of Works, 83–87
Criminal responsibility, Puritan attitude toward, 191–195
Cromwell, Oliver, 37, 111, 154

Davis, James A., xii
Davis, James F., 69
Dennison, Major General, 130–131
Dentler, Robert A., 9
"Deployment patterns," 27–29, 196–199
Depravity, 203
Deviant behavior, viii–ix, 3–29
   definitions, 5–6, 8–9
   Puritan attitude toward, 187–198
   volume of, 23–27, 163–164, 180–181
Devil, the, in Puritan imagery, 64, 157–159
Dickens, Charles, 203
Downing, Emmanuel, 46
Dudley, Thomas, 75, 90, 94–95, 96, 98, 99, 185–186
Durkheim, Emile, 3–5, 8, 26
Dyer, Mary, 120–121, 123

Eastern State Penitentiary (Philadelphia), 200–204
Elizabeth I, 35–36, 44, 47, 154
Ellis, George Edward, 23
Emory University, xiii
Endicott, John, 96, 113–114, 120, 132, 134
Erikson, Erik H., xii, 53–54

Erikson, Joanne, xiii
Erikson, Kai T., 9, 14
Essex County Court, records of, 164–168
Esty, Mary, 145

Felltham, Owen, 45
Felt, Joseph B., 213
Flanders, Jane, 193

Garfinkel, Harold, 16
Geobel, Julius, Jr., 56
Goffman, Erving, 14
Good, Dorcas, 144
Good, Sarah, 143, 144

Hadlock, Nathaniel, 132
Haskins, George L., 56
Hawthorne, Nathaniel, 170, 188
Haynes, John, 75, 186
Heimert, Alan, 140, 157
Henry VIII, 34–35
History, as special discipline, vii–x
Hoar, Dorcas, 145
Hobbs, Abigail, 145
Holland, Bernard C., xii
Howard, John, 15
Hull, John, 125
Hutchinson, Anne, 58, 74, 77–83, 85–91, 106–107, 168, 175
   banishment of, 91–92
   church trial of, 102–105
   civil trial of, 92–101
Hutchinson, Thomas, 77, 92, 122–123, 133, 140
Huxley, Aldous, 13

Independency, in England, 110–111

James I, 36, 45, 46, 48, 51, 154
Janowitz, Morris, xiii
Josselyn, John, 139

Katz, Elihu, xii
King Philip's War, 138, 214, 215

Kitsuse, John I., xii, 6
Kittredge, George L., 153

Lawson, Deodat, 142
Leddra, William, 123, 133
Lemert, Edwin M., 6
Love, Walter D., xii
Luther, Martin, 34, 84, 85
Lynds, Elam, 202–203

Martin, Susanna, 145
Massachusetts Bay, charter of, 37–
    38, 55, 138, 155
  historians of, ix–xi
  legal structure, 54–63
  as object of research, vi–vii
  population of, 213–215
  records of, 109
  trial procedure of, 150–152
Mather, Cotton, 21–22, 74, 133,
    136, 141, 150, 157, 158–159,
    193–194
Mather, Increase, 136
Mead, George Herbert, 4, 8
Mental hospitals, 25
  as agency of control, 8, 14–15
Merton, Robert K., 17, 20
Miller, Perry, xi, 40, 46, 107, 110,
    112–113, 187
Morgan, Edmund S., 64

New England Way, the, 64, 68, 70,
    71–72, 107, 110–111, 126, 136,
    138, 158
Norton, John, 113
Notestein, Wallace, 153
Nurse, Rebecca, 145

Oberholzer, Emil, Jr., 168
Osburne, Sarah, 143, 144
Oyer and Terminer, Court of, 148,
    150, 152

Palfrey, John, 188
Park, Charles E., 126
Parliament, 35, 36, 111

Parris, Samuel, 141, 142, 147
Parsons, Talcott, 15
Peters, Hugh, 95, 96, 97, 185
Phips, Sir William, 148, 150, 152,
    153
Pittsburgh, University of, xiii
Polsby, Nelson, xii
Predestination, 189–192
Prisons, as agency of control, 8, 14–
    15
  in American history, 199–205
Proctor, Elizabeth, 147–148
Proctor, John, 145, 148
Punishment, as deterrent, 24–25
  as public spectacle, 12
  Puritan attitudes toward, 188–191
  as sacrifice, 192, 194–195
Puritanism, attitude toward Bible,
    47, 49–50, 56–58
  effect on American penal methods,
    202–205
  as form of community discipline,
    169–171
  origins in England, 33–37
  as revolutionary movement, 45–46
  as "world view," 44–53
Putnam, Ann, 147–148

Quakers, 107–136, 176–179, 201

Reformation, 83–84
  in English history, 33–37
Robinson, William, 120–121
Rush, Benjamin, 199

Self-fulfilling prophesy, 17
Separatism, 39, 41
Sharp, Geoffrey A., xii
Shattock, Samuel, 131–132
Shaw, George Bernard, 24
Shepard, Thomas, 42
Sociology, as related to history, vii–
    viii, x–xi
  as special discipline, 18–19
Spectral evidence, 151–152
Starkey, Marion L., 70, 137

Steffens, Lincoln, 69
Stevenson, Marmaduke, 120–121
Strauss, Anselm L., xii
Strickland, Charles E., xii
Sykes, Gresham, 14
Synod of 1637, 90–91

Talbye, Dorothy, 193
Teeters, Negley K., 199, 203
Tituba, 141, 143, 144
Tocqueville, Alexis de, 201, 202, 203–204
Toleration, 111–114, 133–134, 136
Trials by test, 151

Vane, Henry, 185–186
    role in Antinomian Controversy, 76–77, 79, 80, 88–90, 111
Vosburg, Robert L., xii

Ward, Nathaniel, 63–64, 111–112
Wertenbaker, Thomas J., 170
Wharton, Edward, 128

Wheelwright, John, 78–80, 88, 90–92
    banishment of, 91–92
Wild, Sarah, 145
Wilderness, as theme in Puritan imagery, 140–141, 157–158
Willard, Samuel, 149
William of Orange, 138
Williams, Abigail, 142, 147
Williams, Roger, 79, 111, 125
Wilson, Deborah, 132
Wilson, John, 120–121
    role in Antinomian Controversy, 75–80, 86, 90, 104, 105
Winthrop, John, v, 37, 51–52, 62, 109–110, 113, 114, 139, 170, 185–187, 191, 193
    role in Antinomian Controversy, 74–78, 80–82, 88–91, 92–102, 105–106
Witchcraft, in England, 153–155
    in New England, 22–23, 137–153, 154–159
Woodhouse, A. S. P., 40